The Ultimate Self-Teaching Method!

Play Ukulele Today!

A Complete Guide to the Basics

PLAYBACK+
Speed • Pitch • Balance • Loop

To access audio and video visit:
www.halleonard.com/mylibrary

Enter Code
6426-4124-2942-0345

by Barrett Tagliarino

Recording Credits:
Barrett Tagliarino, Ukulele & Narration
Scott Houghton, Vocals
Billy Burke, Engineer

ISBN 978-1-5400-5238-4

Visit Hal Leonard Online at
www.halleonard.com

Contact us:
Hal Leonard
7777 West Bluemound Road
Milwaukee, WI 53213
Email: info@halleonard.com

In Europe, contact:
Hal Leonard Europe Limited
42 Wigmore Street
Marylebone, London, W1U 2RN
Email: info@halleonardeurope.com

In Australia, contact:
Hal Leonard Australia Pty. Ltd.
4 Lentara Court
Cheltenham, Victoria, 3192 Australia
Email: info@halleonard.com.au

Introduction

Track 1

Welcome to *Play Ukulele Today!*—This book is designed to get you started on this fun and easy instrument, with everything you need to know to play chords and melodies, and to learn songs you can sing and play.

About the Audio & Video

The accompanying audio will take you step by step through each lesson and play each example. Much like with a real lesson, the best way to learn this material is to read and practice a while at first on your own, then listen to the audio. With *Play Ukulele Today!*, you can learn at your own pace. If there is ever something that you don't quite understand the first time through, go back and listen to the track number listed to replay the teacher's explanation. Every musical track has been given its own track number, so if you want to practice a song again, you can find it right away.

On musical examples, the audio has been mixed with the chords on the left channel, and the melody on the right channel. To practice playing chords beneath the melody, adjust the balance to the right on your playback device. To practice the melody using the chord accompaniment only, adjust the balance to the left. On most single-instrument examples, a metronome or "click track" is used to keep time. The click is often "panned" on the opposite side of the ukulele in the stereo field, so you can practice with as much or as little of the recorded ukulele as you need to hear to help keep your place.

Some lessons in the book include video lessons, so you can see and hear the material being taught. Audio and videos are indicated with icons.

 Audio Icon   Video Icon

Contents

The Basics

The Parts of the Ukulele

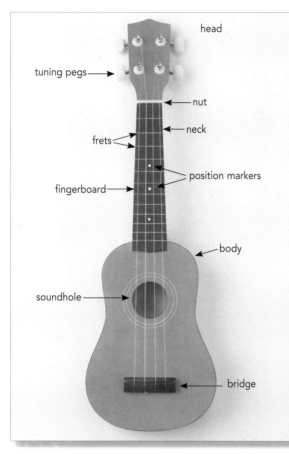

head

tuning pegs →

nut

neck

frets

position markers

fingerboard →

body

soundhole

bridge

Ukuleles come in four sizes: **soprano**, **concert**, **tenor**, and **baritone**.

A **soprano ukulele** is usually about 21 inches long. The **concert** size is about 23 inches and is tuned the same as the soprano. The soprano is most popular and is probably what you have if you're not sure. This book is designed for use with soprano and concert ukuleles and banjo ukuleles.

The **tenor ukulele**, at 26 inches long, is tuned like the soprano and concert except that the fourth string, G, is an octave lower. (Octaves are discussed in the section on music reading.) This book may be applied to the tenor with slight considerations made for the G string.

Baritone ukuleles are the largest at 30 inches and are tuned similarly to the tenor ukulele but a 4th lower. Using this book with a baritone will require *transposition*, especially if you plan to play with other instruments.

How to Hold Your Ukulele

Stand or sit up straight (but not stiff) and support the body of the ukulele with your right forearm. This "arm grip" should be loose enough to allow you to easily strum the strings with your right thumb and fingers. Support the neck at a slight upward angle between your left-hand thumb and first finger. This grip should also be free and easy, to allow your hand to move up or down the neck to any fingerboard position.

Left-handed players may reverse these instructions, as well as restringing and tuning their instruments to be a mirror image of the diagrams. Many lefties decide to go ahead and play right-handed. This is OK—the left (fretting) hand has the most complicated job anyway.

Your Right and Left Hands

Your left-hand fingers are numbered 1 through 4.

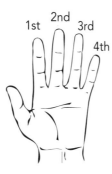

Place the thumb in back of the neck roughly opposite the second finger. Avoid letting your palm touch the back of the neck.

Strum the ukulele in the area where the neck joins the body. This will give the best tone. Don't strum over the sound hole, unless your left hand is playing high up on the neck. In general, strum downward with the thumb and up with the first finger.

Many ukulele players get a nice clear sound by playing with a stiff felt pick. Hold the pick between your crossed thumb and first finger with the point of the pick extending beyond the tip of the first finger.

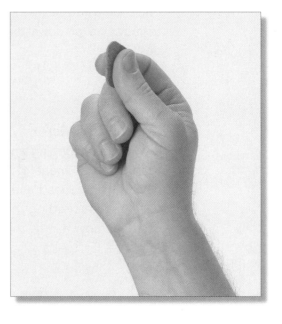

Playing Is Easy

The ukulele strings are numbered 1 to 4, with string number 1 being closest to the floor. That's opposite what you might think—the fourth string is the one closest to your nose.

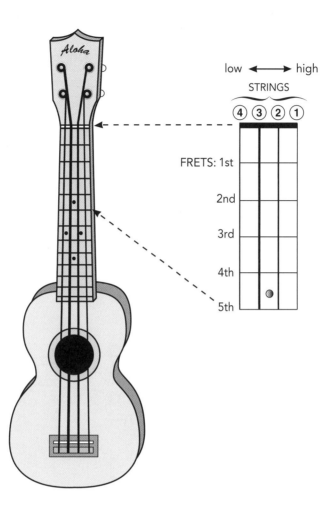

Also notice that fret numbers go up as they get closer to the body of the ukulele. If you play on the higher frets, your hand is said to be moving "up" the neck.

Tuning Up

If you loosen a string by turning its tuning key, the pitch will become lower. If you tighten the string, the pitch will become higher. When two pitches sound exactly the same, they are said to be *in tune*.

Some tuning keys have a small adjustment screw in the end. If your ukulele strings keep going out of tune on you, it's possible this screw may need to be carefully tightened by turning it clockwise. This is a screw you don't want to strip, so just tighten it enough so that the key stays where you put it. If the key is difficult to turn, you may try slightly loosening this screw.

Tuning to the Audio

Track 5 will play the correct pitch of each string, starting with string number 4. While plucking each string to hear its pitch, carefully adjust the tension to match the pitch on the track. Higher tension produces higher notes. If you over-tighten the string you may break it; but don't worry, it happens to everyone, and strings are inexpensive.

When a string is too tight, the pitch produced is said to be "sharp." A too-loose string is said to be "flat." The strings of a tuned ukulele produce a little melody:

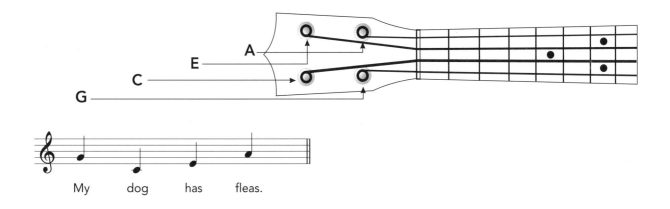

You can also tune to a pitch pipe or an electronic tuner. Both are available at music stores and come with instructions.

Here are a few tips to help get you started:

- Whether tightening or loosening a string, turn the key slowly so that you can concentrate on the changes in pitch. Ukulele notes fade away quickly, so you will need to pluck the string repeatedly to compare it to your tuning reference.

- Instead of tuning a sharp string down to pitch, tune it up. Tuning up allows the string tension to remove the play between the tuning peg gears, which will help the string stay in tune longer. So if you begin with a string that is sharp (too high in pitch), tune it down first (so that it's flat), and then bring it back up to pitch.

Tuning to Other Instruments

Instruments that will be played together should all be tuned to a similar reference. In this age of digital perfection, this is not so hard to achieve anymore, but you may still have to tune to a piano or another instrument that is not at concert pitch.

The ukulele's third string, C, corresponds to middle C on the piano.

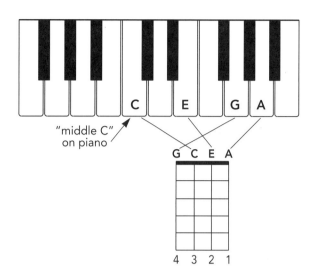

Relative Tuning of the Strings

If you know that one string is correctly tuned, you can use it to tune the others. This method, *relative tuning*, is vital for quickly checking that the ukulele is in tune (at least with itself) at any time. Here's how:

- Let's assume that the third string is correctly tuned to C. You can start with whichever string you think is closest to being in tune once you understand the system. We'll start with C because it's the lowest available note on the ukulele.

- Press the third string at the seventh fret. This is the pitch G, to which you tune the open (unfretted) fourth string. Play the two notes together and adjust the fourth string until the two strings match.

- Now press the third string at the fourth fret. This is the pitch E, to which you tune your open second string. Play the two notes together, adjusting the open second string until it matches the fretted note on the third string.

- Finally, press the second string at the fifth fret. The open first string, A, should be tuned to match this note.

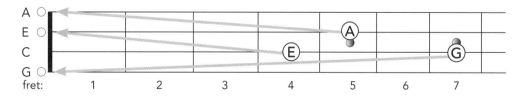

Track 5

Tuning Notes

How to Read Music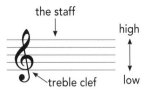

Track 6

Pitch

Music is written in **notes** on a **staff**. The staff has five lines with four spaces between them. Where a note is written on the staff determines its **pitch** (highness or lowness).

At the beginning of the staff is a **clef sign**. Most melodies are written in the **treble clef**.

Each line and space of the staff has a letter name. The lines are (from bottom to top) **E–G–B–D–F**, which you can remember as **E**very **G**ood **B**oy **D**oes **F**ine. The spaces are (from bottom to top) **F–A–C–E**, which spells "**Face**."

The lines and spaces together spell the **musical alphabet** using the first seven letters of the English alphabet, A through G. Once G is reached, the musical alphabet starts over. Two different notes with the same letter name—for instance, E on the first line and E on the fourth space—are said to be an **octave** (eight notes) apart.

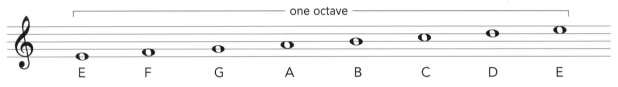

Rhythm

The staff is divided into several parts by **bar lines**. The space between two bar lines is called a **measure** (also known as a "bar"). To end a piece of music, a **double bar line** is placed on the staff.

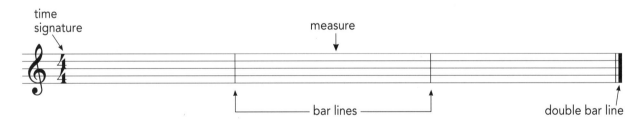

Each measure contains a group of **beats**. Beats are the steady pulse of music. You respond to the pulse or beat when you tap your foot. The **time signature** tells you how many beats are in a measure.

Notes indicate the length (number of counts) of musical sound.

You can tell which pitch to play by the position of a note on the staff and how to long to play it by its shape.

8

Playing Chords

Track 7

The ukulele's role is most often to play *chords*, which provide accompaniment for singing or another instrument carrying the melody. Chords consist of two or more notes strummed at the same time. In fact, most ukulele chords use all four strings, making the "uke" easy and fun to play.

To play a chord, first get your left-hand fingers into position. The dots on each grid tell you where to fret the strings, and the numbers tell you which fingers to use. Depress the strings with the tips of your fingers, and arch your fingers to avoid touching strings that are to be played open. Strum the strings with a downward motion of your thumb or pick. All strings should sound as one—not separately.

C

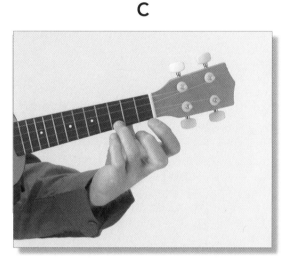

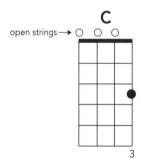

G7

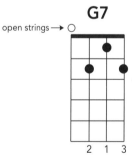

► Keep your left-hand fingernails trimmed for easier fretting.

Slash Rhythms

Chord symbols are written above the staff, and **slash rhythms** show when the chords are strummed and how long to let them ring. Slash rhythms cover the middle two spaces of the staff to let you know chords are to be played instead of single notes. No clef sign is necessary when writing slash rhythms, since they don't indicate pitch.

Often simple slash marks with no stems are used, which tells you to "play time" in the style of the piece. For the ukulele, we can usually interpret this to mean the same as the quarter-note slash rhythm: four strums per measure.

Practice the following exercise strumming once for each slash mark, using downstrokes only. Keep a steady beat, and change chord fingerings as quickly as you can.

Track 8

C-G7

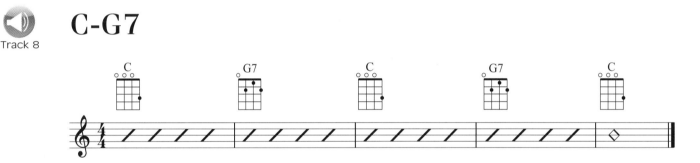

As you practice the transition between these chords, you may notice that there's no need to lift the third finger off the fretboard. That's a good thing! Keep the third finger down and just **slide** it from the third to the second fret when going from C to G7. Then slide the third finger back up to the third fret when changing from G7 to C.

Now apply the same "quarter-note strum" to the song below, playing along with the track.

Track 9

Strum-a-Thon

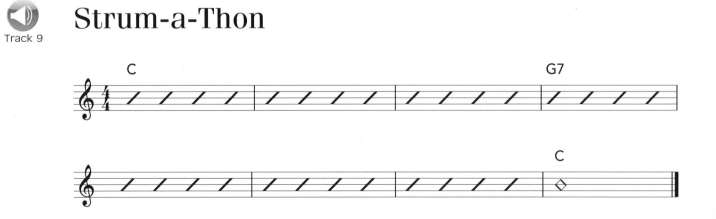

Now let's add two more chords to your repertoire: G and D7.

G

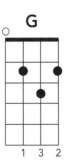

D7

The D7 is our first *barre* chord. For barre chords, your finger must flatten out across multiple strings. All the strings should be pressed into solid contact with the fret to make a clear sound when you strum the chord. For this particular chord, the first string is also played by the second finger, one fret higher than the first, so it doesn't matter if your barre covers the first string.

Don't give up if you can't play the barre chord at first—practice makes perfect. Just try your best, and let your fingers adapt to the new position over time.

Track 10

Step Up to the Barre

▶ As you're learning new chords, pluck each string of the chord individually to make sure the notes are fretted properly.

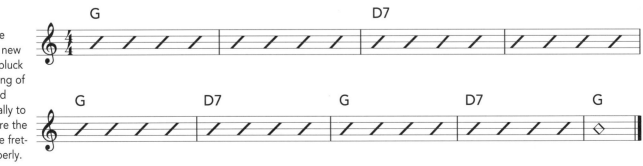

Keeping Time

Having trouble keeping a steady rhythm? Tap your foot and count out loud. Each time the foot comes down marks one beat. In 4/4 time, tap your foot four times in each measure, and count "1, 2, 3, 4." The first beat of each new measure should be accented slightly—this is indicated below by the symbol ">."

Review the fingering for the C chord and then practice this exercise until you can play it well.

Track 11

Chord Study

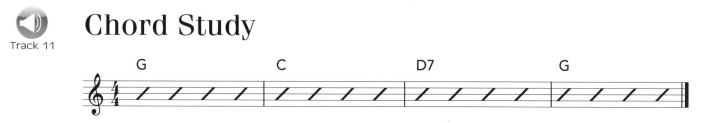

Tracks 12–14 use the four chords you have learned so far. The chords are arranged in sequences called *chord progressions*.

Track 12

Progression 1

Now try switching between these chords in different sequences and rhythms.

Track 13

Progression 2

Track 14

Progression 3

Two New Chords: F and A

Track 15

F

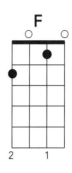

A

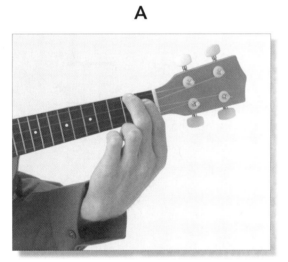

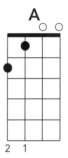

Track 16
slow/fast

Barbershop

► Remember to arch your fingers to allow the open strings of a chord to ring out properly.

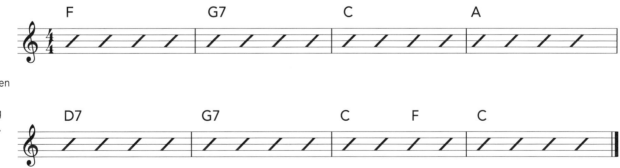

Notes on the First String: A

Track 17

In addition to chords, you can also play melodies on the ukulele by using one string at a time. Start by playing all downstrokes with the thumb or pick. Later we'll add upstrokes with the first finger or pick. Use whichever you prefer; you may find the pick gives a cleaner sound, especially when playing upstrokes.

A

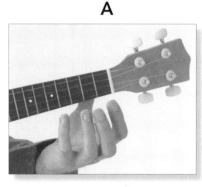

■ Your first note, A, is an "open-string" tone. There's nothing to fret—simply pluck (or pick) the open first string.

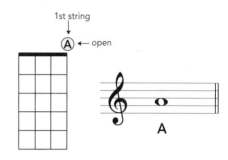

B

■ For the next note, B, place your second finger on the second fret of the first string and pluck.

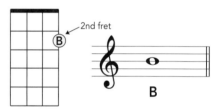

C

► Remember, your finger belongs directly behind the metal fret. If you place it on top of the fret, or too far back, you'll have difficulty getting a clear sound.

■ To play C, place your third finger on the third fret and pluck the first string.

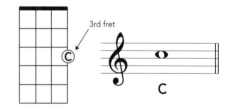

Learn to recognize these notes both on the fretboard and on the staff. Then, when you're comfortable playing the notes individually, try this short exercise. Speak the note names aloud as you play (e.g., "A, B, C, B...").

Track 18

A-B-C

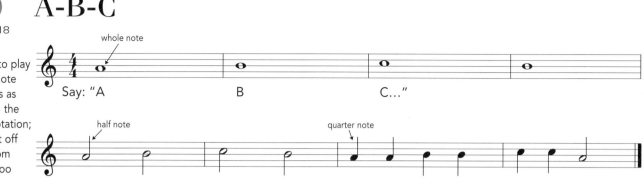

► Be sure to play the full note durations as shown in the music notation; don't cut off notes from ringing too early.

Of course, the best way to really learn these notes is to use them in some tunes. Start slowly with the following melodies, and keep your pace nice and even.

Track 19

First Melody

Steady rhythm when playing single notes is just as important as when playing chords. Again, tap your foot on each beat and count along with all four beats in each measure.

Second Melody

Track 20

Third Melody

Track 21

► It's also good practice to read through each song without your ukulele first: tap the beat with your foot, count aloud, and clap through the rhythms.

Sharps, Flats, and Naturals

Sharps and flats are part of a group of musical symbols called **accidentals**, which raise or lower the pitch of a note:

A **sharp** (♯) raises the pitch of a note by one fret.

A **flat** (♭) lowers the pitch of a note by one fret.

A **natural** (♮) cancels a previous sharp or flat, returning a note to its original pitch.

In musical terms, the distance of one fret is called a **half step**. When a song requires a note to be a half step higher or lower, you'll see a sharp (♯), flat (♭), or natural (♮) sign in front of it.

Track 22

Two New Notes: B♭ and C♯

These are notes named with **accidentals**, between the natural notes we've already learned.

B♭

► This is one fret *lower* than the B note you already learned.

■ For the note B-flat (B♭), place your first finger on the first fret and pluck the first string.

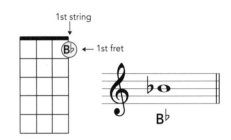

C♯

► This is one fret *higher* than the C note you already learned.

■ To play C-sharp (C♯), place your fourth finger on the fourth fret and pluck the first string.

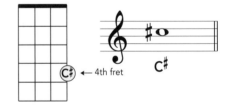

Accidentals apply only throughout the measure in which they appear. An accidental must be restated if the melody uses it again in a later measure.

Track 23

B♭-C♯

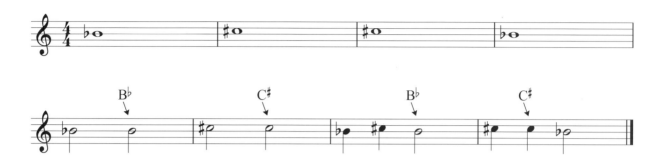

Here is a tune to practice all five notes we've learned so far. Don't be afraid to review the A, B, and C notes again before tackling this one!

Track 24

Play It!

▶ Watch out for the natural sign!

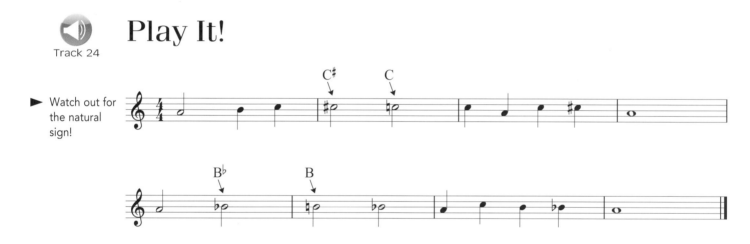

Notes on the Second String: E

Track 25

Your next three notes are all played on the second string, E. You might want to check your tuning on that string before going any farther.

E

■ To play the note E, just pluck the open second string.

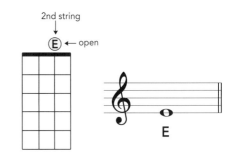

F

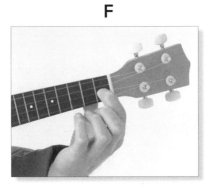

■ To play the note F, place your first finger on the first fret of the second string.

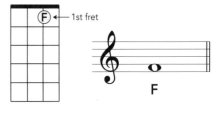

G

■ To play the note G, place your third finger on the third fret of the second string.

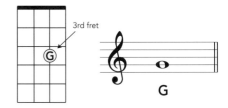

Track 26

Second-String Study

Here's a single-note melody that uses notes we have learned on the first and second strings.

Naturals

Track 27

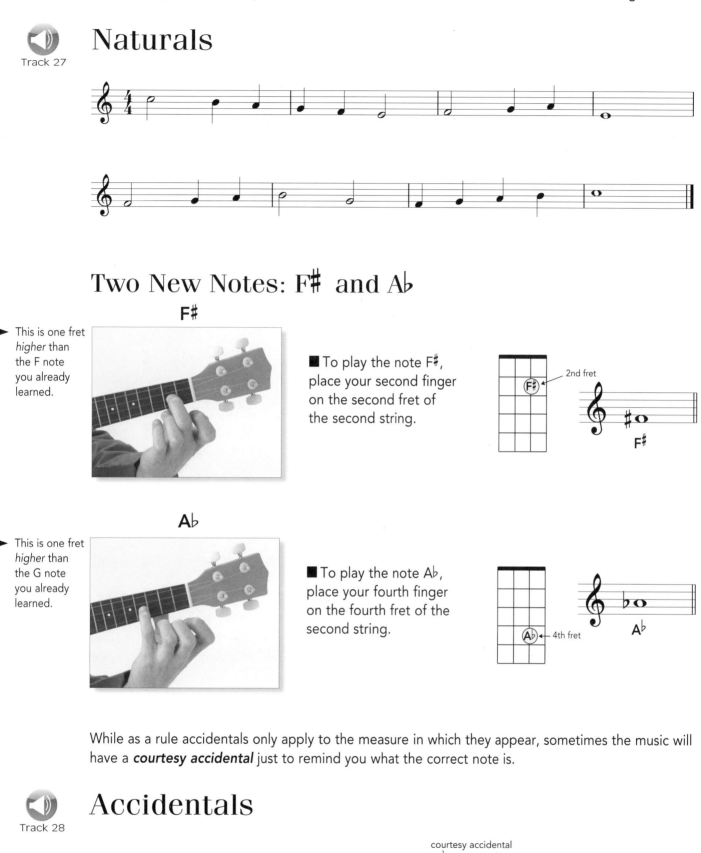

Two New Notes: F# and A♭

F#

► This is one fret *higher* than the F note you already learned.

■ To play the note F#, place your second finger on the second fret of the second string.

2nd fret

A♭

► This is one fret *higher* than the G note you already learned.

■ To play the note A♭, place your fourth finger on the fourth fret of the second string.

4th fret

While as a rule accidentals only apply to the measure in which they appear, sometimes the music will have a **courtesy accidental** just to remind you what the correct note is.

Accidentals

Track 28

courtesy accidental

Enharmonic Equivalents

The next song has a "new" note, G♯. G♯ is really a note you already know as A♭. How can one note have two names? It just depends on which way you approach it: up from G or down from A. Notes like G♯ and A♭ are called **enharmonic equivalents**—a fancy way of saying "two names for the same pitch."

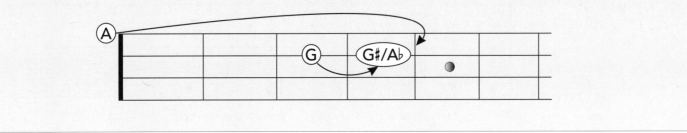

Track 29

Gee, My New Friend Is Sharp

You can read and play a written vocal melody on the ukulele. When the melody becomes familiar (or if it's one you already know), sing it while you strum the chords.

Mary Had a Little Lamb

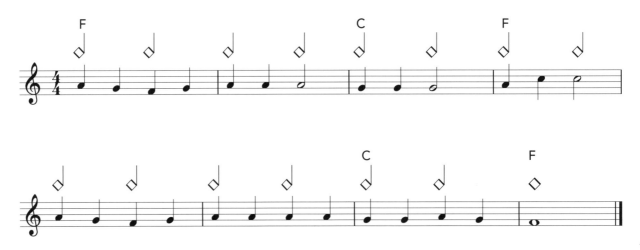

Notes on the Third String: C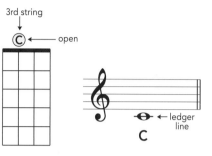

Track 30

Your next two notes are played on the third string, C. The third string will be the last string we'll use to read single notes on soprano and concert ukuleles.

Our new notes on the third string are below the range of the staff in treble clef. If a note is too low or high to fit on the lines or spaces of the staff, we use **ledger lines**, which extend the staff downward or upward.

C

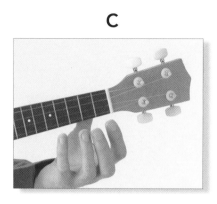

■ To play the note C, just pluck the open third string.

D

■ To play the note D, place your second finger on the second fret of the third string.

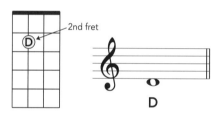

Practice reading the two new notes.

C-D

Here is an exercise that uses the natural notes we've learned on the top three strings.

All Natural

Track 31

Accidentals on the Third String: C♯ and E♭

C♯ (D♭)

■ To play the note C♯ (or its enharmonic equivalent, D♭), place your first finger on the first fret of the third string.

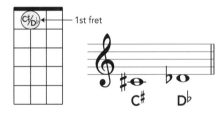

D♯ (E♭)

■ To play the note E♭ (or its enharmonic equivalent, D♯), place your third finger on the third fret of the third string.

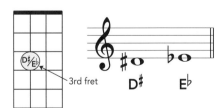

Reading Rhythms

Track 32

Introducing Rests

In addition to notes, songs may also contain silences, or **rests**—beats in which you play or sing nothing at all. A rest is a musical pause. Rests are like notes in that they have their own rhythmic values, instructing you how long (or for how many beats) to pause:

whole rest
(four beats)

half rest
(two beats)

quarter rest
(one beat)

You should stop any previous notes or chords from ringing during a rest. To do this, you will need to use **string damping**:

- After a note or chord, decrease the pressure of your fretting-hand finger(s) on the strings— but don't let go of the neck completely. Let your fretting-hand fingers **damp** (lightly touch) all the strings to stop their vibrations.

- You can also play a rest by damping all the strings with the palm of your strumming hand.

Play the chords shown.

Track 33

Slash Rhythms With Rests

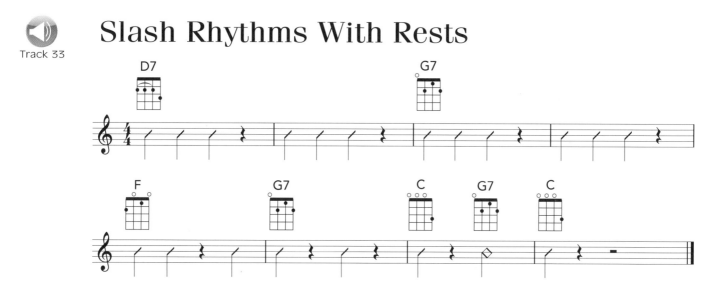

Single-Note Melody With Rests

Track 34

► Try to look a little ahead as you play.

Introducing Eighth Notes

If you divide a quarter note in half, what you get is an *eighth note*. An eighth note looks like a quarter note, but with a flag on its stem.

Two eighth notes equal one quarter note. To help you keep track of the beat, consecutive eighth notes are connected with a beam instead of having flags.

To count eighth notes, divide the beat into two, and use "and" between the beats. Practice this first by counting aloud while tapping your foot on the beat, and then by playing the notes while counting and tapping.

Track 35

1 &   2   &   3   &   4   &   1   &   2   &   3   &   4   &
"and"

Eighth rests are counted the same way, but you pause instead of playing.

1   &   2   &   3   &   4   &   1   &   2   &   3   &   4   &

24

Alternating Downstrokes and Upstrokes

For any measure where you strum chords using eighth-note rhythms, alternate between strumming down with your thumb on the beat and up with your index finger on the "and." This is a little tricky at first, so go super slow.

If you are using a pick to strum the chords, the same principle of alternating up and downstrokes applies.

Track 36

Eighth-Note Rhythm

► Keep your hand moving up and down with your foot even when you are just waiting to play a note. It helps you stay in time.

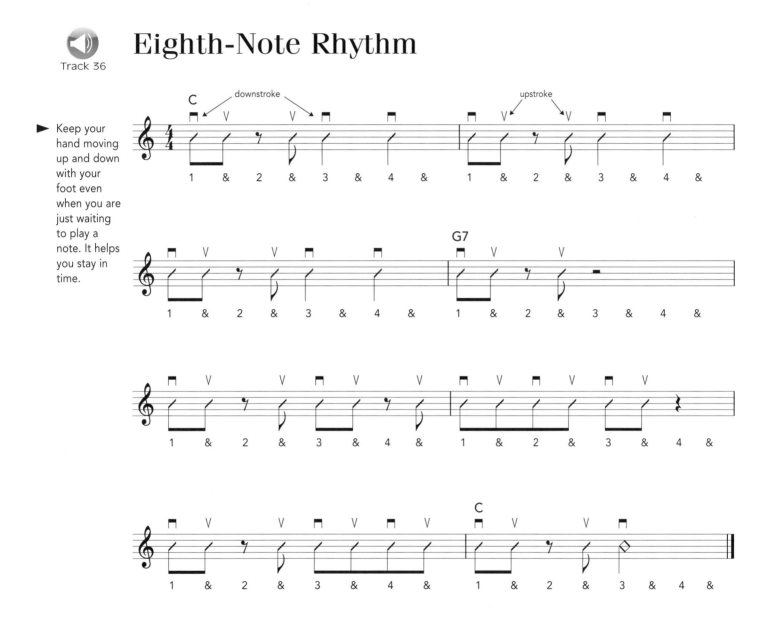

Minor Chords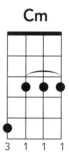

Track 37

When a chord was named with only a letter, it was really just short for a name such as **F major** or **F maj**. Now we have some **minor chords**, which must always have **m** in the symbol.

Cm

Cm

3 1 1 1

Em

Em

3 4 2 1

Let's try out these minor chords in some familiar music. First play the simple melody of "Joshua Fought the Battle of Jericho," then strum the chords in steady quarter notes. This melody includes a note we haven't played before—E♭ on the third fret of the third string.

Track 38

Joshua Fought the Battle of Jericho

3rd string
3rd fret

Repeat signs () tell you to repeat everything in between them. If only one sign appears (:||), repeat from the beginning of the piece.

Track 39

Doo-Wop

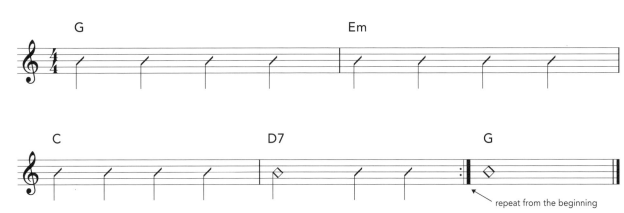

repeat from the beginning

Track 40

3/4 Time

The next song is in **3/4** meter. This means there are three beats (quarter notes) per measure.

3/4 time feels very different from 4/4 time. A song in 3/4 is often called a **waltz**. Be sure to accent the first beat of each measure just slightly; this will help you feel the new meter.

Introducing the Pickup

Instead of starting a song with a rest, a **pickup measure** may be used. A pickup measure is an incomplete measure that deletes any opening rests. So, if a pickup to a song in 4/4 has only one beat, you count "1, 2, 3," and start playing on beat 4.

"Clementine" is a waltz that includes a new (but easy) chord for us, C7. Notice the pickup measure: the melody begins on beat 3. The first chord starts on beat 1. Chord diagrams are included to show the new chord, C7, and to refresh your memory of F and C.

Practice the chords until you can strum throughout the whole song without stopping. Then play the melody on your ukulele. Finally, strum the chords while singing the song.

Track 41

Clementine

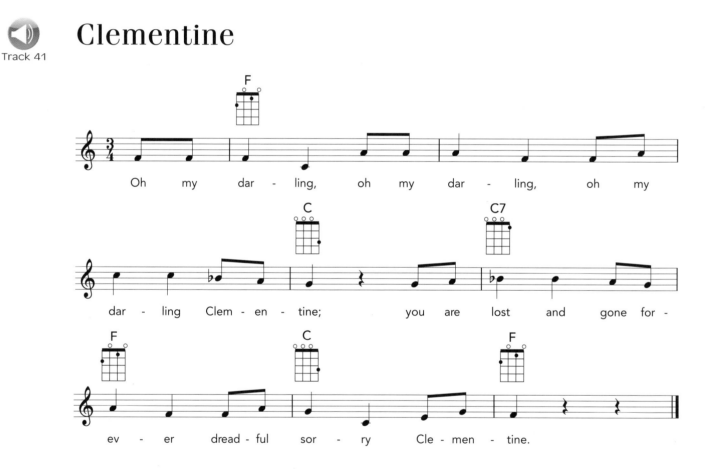

28

Ties and Dots

The *tie* is a curved line that connects two notes of the same pitch. When you see a tie, play the first note and then hold it for the total value of both notes.

Track 42

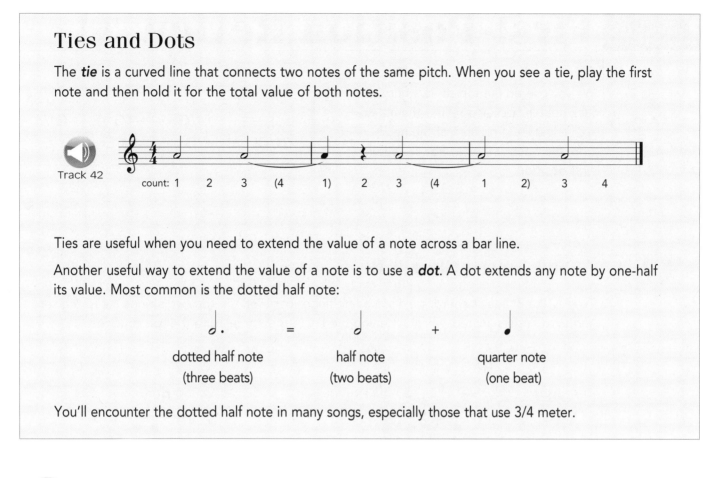

count: 1 2 3 (4 1) 2 3 (4 1 2) 3 4

Ties are useful when you need to extend the value of a note across a bar line.

Another useful way to extend the value of a note is to use a *dot*. A dot extends any note by one-half its value. Most common is the dotted half note:

dotted half note   =   half note   +   quarter note
(three beats)   (two beats)   (one beat)

You'll encounter the dotted half note in many songs, especially those that use 3/4 meter.

Dot's Right

Track 43

First-Position Review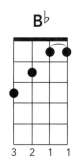

We've covered the top three strings, but let's double back and review the notes we've learned. This area of the neck—from the open strings to fret 4—is called *first position*.

A	A#/B♭	B	C	C#/D♭
E	F	F#/G♭	G	G#/A♭
C	C#/D♭	D	D#/E♭	E
G				

A New Barre Chord: B♭

To play the B♭ major chord, we'll use a first-finger barre on the top two strings. Keep the second and third fingers arched, while flattening the first finger by relaxing the last knuckle.

B♭

Notice the similarity in the shape of the B♭ chord to A when you play this exercise.

It's Fab!

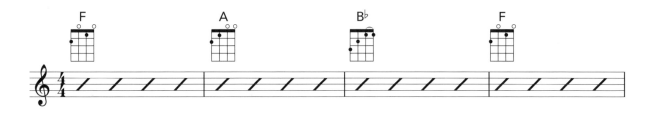

Notes at the Fifth Fret

Although the ukulele is so small you can reach notes on the fifth fret by slightly stretching, it's easier to keep your place by following the "one finger per fret" rule. If you move your first finger to the second fret, your left hand is now said to be in *second position*, and the notes at the fifth fret will be played with your fourth finger.

D

► Remember to anchor your thumb on the back of the neck roughly the opposite of your middle finger.

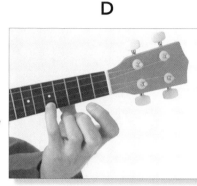

■ To play the high D note, place your fourth finger at the fifth fret of the first string.

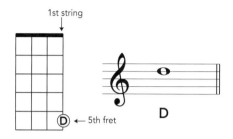

A

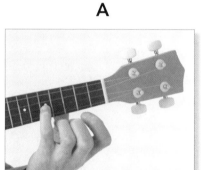

■ To play the A note, place your fourth finger at the fifth fret of the second string.

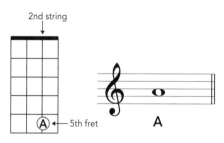

F

■ To play the F note, place your fourth finger at the fifth fret of the third string.

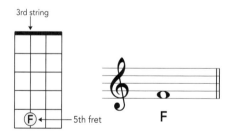

Let's use the notes we just learned to play "Amazing Grace." Keep your first finger on the second fret; however, for smoothness, use the fourth finger for the A note and the *third* finger for the F note on the fifth fret.

Remember to count three beats for each measure, starting the melody on beat 3 of the pickup measure. Then practice the chords, counting each measure of 3/4 time aloud. Finally, strum the chords in quarter notes, and sing the lyrics to this classic song.

Track 47

Amazing Grace

There's More Than One Place to Find a Note

The lowest notes we can play, on frets 0 (open) through 3 of the third string, are only available in first position. But the other notes we've learned may also be found higher up the neck on lower strings.

For instance, the note E, which we learned as the open second string, may also be fretted at the fourth fret of the third string. Also, we now have two places to play F and A.

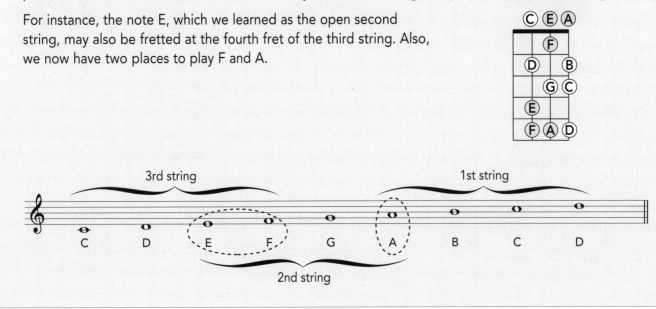

32

Jumping Octaves

Much of the ukulele's appeal stems from its very high range of notes. But we only have three strings on which to read melodies, which is less than most stringed instruments. As a result, sometimes it's necessary to play notes an **octave** (eight notes) higher or lower than written when reading, then remember to switch them back when singing.

Here's an example. "Shalom Chaverim" starts on B *below the staff*, which is lower than we can play. But that doesn't mean we can't learn the song! We'll read the B an octave higher, on the second fret of the first string. Let's also drop the high E in measure 3 down by an octave, playing it on the open second string.

Shalom Chaverim

Major Scales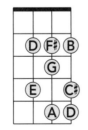

Now it's time to start learning about scales. "What's a scale?" you ask. A **scale** is an arrangement of notes in a specific, sequential pattern. Most scales use eight notes, with the top and bottom notes being an octave apart.

Two things give a scale its name: its lowest note (called the root), and the pattern of whole and half steps it uses. (A **whole step** is two frets; a **half step** is one fret.)

A **major** scale is always built using this interval formula:

whole – whole – half – whole – whole – whole – half

Let's take a look at some major scales!

► Notice that in a C major scale, there are only natural notes: no sharps or flats.

The C Major Scale

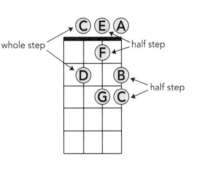

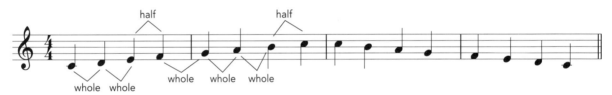

► Notice that in a D major scale, there are two sharps: F♯ and C♯.

The D Major Scale

Movable Major Scale Forms

Track 50

Any scale pattern that does not use open strings can be used all over the neck to play scales from different roots. For instance, just find the desired root note on string 3 or 2, then apply one of the patterns below—and there's your scale.

Root on the Third String

► The circled dots in the diagram represent the root note of the major scale form.

Root on the Second String

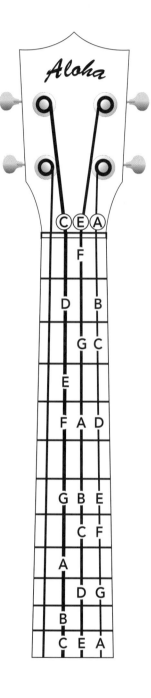

With moveable scale forms we can start on any of the twelve possible roots. Let's do just that to play some major scales. We can play an F major scale in fifth position, starting with the root on the third string, fifth fret. The highest note will be F on the eighth fret of the first string.

Track 51

The F Major Scale

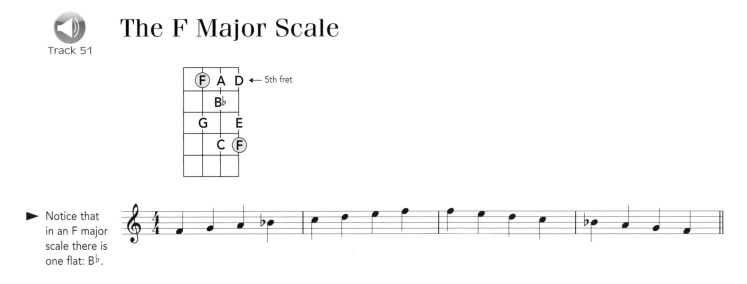

► Notice that in an F major scale there is one flat: B♭.

We can play an A major scale in fourth position, starting with the second finger on the second string, fifth fret. The highest note in the fingering pattern is E on the seventh fret of the first string. When practicing a pattern like this one (where there are notes included below the root), start on the root, play to the highest note, and then descend to the lowest note. Then climb back up and finish the scale on the root to help reinforce its sound to your ear.

Remember to start with the second (middle) finger.

Track 52

The A Major Scale

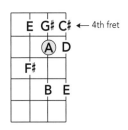

► Notice that in an A major scale there are three sharps: F♯, C♯, and G♯.

Key Signatures

In written music, a **key signature** is found at the beginning of the staff, between the clef and the time signature. It defines what notes will be sharp or flat—or essentially, what key you'll be playing in.

Key of E, four sharps

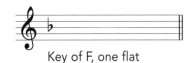

Key of F, one flat

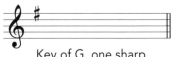

Key of G, one sharp

So What's a Key?

Good question. **Key** and *scale* are almost the same thing. When we know a scale—like E major—we have all the notes we need to play in the corresponding key—E major!

Keys have two components in common with scales:

1) A root, or *tonic*, which is the defining note. This is often (but not always) the first or last note in a piece of music, and it usually feels the most resolved, or "at rest."

2) A *quality*. In this case, a major scale corresponds to a major key.

Track 53

G's the Key

▶ Watch the key signature; it tells you what notes to play sharp (or flat) throughout the song.

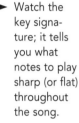
Track 54

Red River Valley

Come and sit by my side if you love me. Do not

hast - en to bid me a - dieu. But re -

mem - ber the Red Riv - er Val - ley, and the

cow - boy who loved you so true.

Home on the Range

Minor Scales

Track 56

We've checked out some major scales. A minor scale has a different interval formula:

whole – half – whole – whole – half – whole – whole

Let's look at some minor scales on the staff and the ukulele fingerboard.

C Minor

Track 57

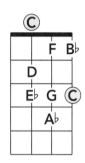

► Notice that in a C minor scale there are three flats: B♭, E♭, and A♭.

D Minor

Track 58

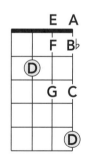

► Notice that in a D minor scale there is only one flat: B♭.

Movable Minor Scale Forms

These shapes produce a minor scale from whichever root they're started on. Again, locate the desired root, and voilà!—as if by magic, a minor scale in any key you need.

Root on the Third String

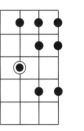

Root on the Second String

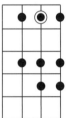

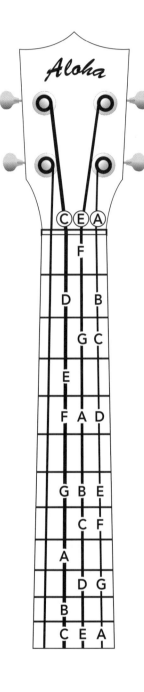

Major vs. Minor

The difference between major and minor scales is not just about whole and half steps—it's about how they *sound*. Take a minute to compare a major and a minor scale—like C major and C minor. Notice how each makes you feel? It's difficult to put into words, but generally we say that major scales (and keys) have a strong, upbeat, or happy quality, while minor scales and keys have a darker, sadder quality.

E Minor Tragedy

Track 59

G Minor Blues

Track 60

Two New Chords: Dm and Am

Our next tune features two minor chords, Dm and Am. Let's practice these new chords first.

Dm

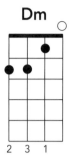

Am

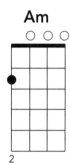

Track 61

Drunken Sailor

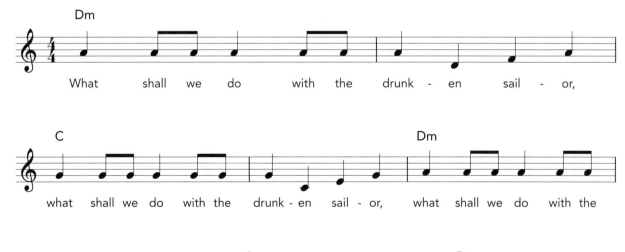

What shall we do with the drunk - en sail - or,

what shall we do with the drunk - en sail - or, what shall we do with the

drunk - en sail - or, ear - ly in the morn - ing?

This page intentionally left blank.

Review

Track 62

So far, you've learned the parts of the ukulele, how to hold your ukulele, the fundamentals of reading music, how to play simple chords and melodies, general thumb and finger strumming, and the use of a felt pick. Major and minor scales were covered, as well as all the notes on the first three strings up to the fifth fret, encompassing first and second positions. Now, we shall take time to briefly review these notes and positions.

Review of First and Second Position

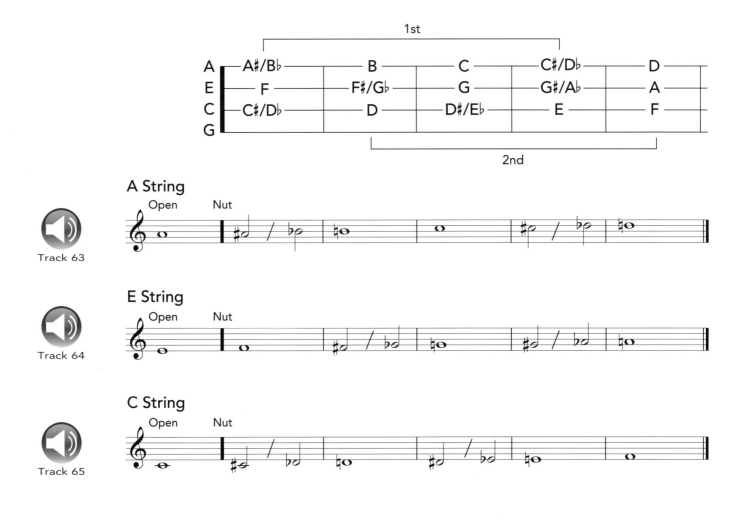

Track 63

Track 64

Track 65

Position Playing

Position playing is a system where your fingers cover the frets in succession. The position you're in is determined by the fret at which the first finger (index) is anchored. For example, in *first* position your index finger is located at the first fret, middle finger at the second fret, ring finger at the third fret, and pinky at the fourth fret.

Starting with first position, let's play a couple of chromatic exercises to cover all of these notes in order. Below is a chromatic scale, starting on C.

Chromatic Scale

A *chromatic scale* or 12-tone scale contains all twelve pitches of the Western scale. It's made up entirely of half steps, or semi-tones, and proceeds from one half step to the next. It could be considered the scale from which all others are derived.

Typically, sharped notes are used when ascending, and flatted notes are used when descending.

Chromatic Scale

Track 66

Ascending Chromatic Scale

Descending Chromatic Scale

This next exercise will cover all the notes and fingerings possible on the first three strings in first position.

First Down Flat

Track 67

Picking Melodies

When picking single note melody lines with your right (or picking) hand, you may choose from a few methods:

- Downstrokes of the thumb – this provides a nice, strong tone. However, in faster tempos, this may become awkward.

- Picking down with the thumb and up with the index finger – this works great for faster tunes and passages.

- Pick alternating upstrokes with the first and second fingers – this method is used extensively by classical and flamenco guitarists.

- Alternating downstrokes and upstrokes with the first finger or thumb, using it like a pick – this method is a bit unorthodox, but worthy of experimentation.

Now that we've reviewed the notes in first position, let's try a few tunes!

Track 68

Beautiful Dreamer

Beau - ti - ful dream - er, wake un - to me.____

Star - light and dew drops are wait - ing for thee.____

Sounds of the rude world, heard in the day,____

lulled by the moon - light have all passed a - way!____

Track 69

New Chord: Gm

Gm

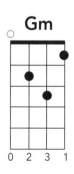

Gm

0 2 3 1

46

In addition to the new Gm chord, this beautiful piece provides a great review of first-position notes, as well as a revisiting of a variety of chords. The changes are frequent, so take it nice and easy with even quarter-note downstrokes of the thumb.

O Come, O Come Immanuel

Track 70

Now, let's take a look at second position. Remember to start with your first finger at the second fret.

Spider Walk

Track 71

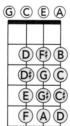

2nd Position

47

Here's a familiar melody that you may play entirely in the second position.

Itsy Bitsy Spider

Track 72

► Remember to play the A note at fret 5 on the second string with your fourth finger.

If we add one note to the "Spider Walk" pattern at the first fret, first string (A♯ or B♭), we get a movable chromatic scale.

Movable Chromatic Scale

Track 73

Movable
Chromatic Pattern

48

To play "In the Hall of the Mountain King," we'll start in first position, switch briefly to second position at the end of measures 3 and 7, and then return to first position to complete measures 4 and 8.

With regards to chords, this song has a couple we have not seen before: E and E♭. This is a closed chord form, which makes it movable, thus enabling it to be used for different chords as it's moved up the neck. From E, the E♭ is the same form, but one fret down.

Track 74

New Chords: E and E♭

E

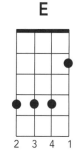

E♭

In this next song, your second and third fingers should maintain their placement on the 4th and 3rd strings as you move between the Dm, E, and E♭ chords.

Track 75

In the Hall of the Mountain King

► Note that the open A string, just before and after the position shifts, gives us a smooth transfer point to make the shifts.

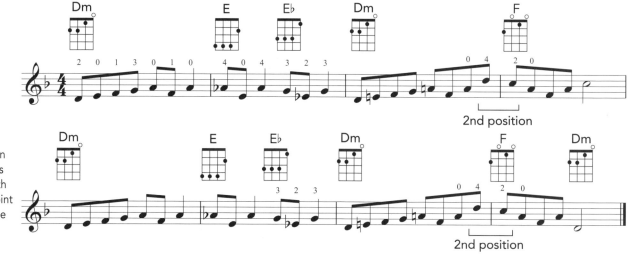

Notes on the Fourth String: G

Track 76

Earlier in this book, we covered all the notes in both first and second position on the first, second, and third strings. This gives us a good understanding of how the notes progress on a linear level. For a more thorough knowledge of the instrument, we must also become familiar with the notes on the fourth string, G. This will not only help our chord playing, but also our melodic playing as we delve into fingerstyle.

G

■ To play G, pluck the open fourth string.

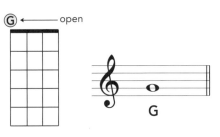

A

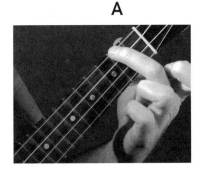

■ To play A, place your second finger at the second fret of the fourth string.

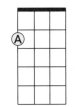

B

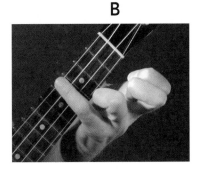

■ To play B, place your fourth finger at the fourth fret of the fourth string.

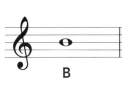

These are notes we already know, but, as is the case with most of the notes on the instrument, they can be found in more than one place. G is the same note as fret 3 on string 2, and A is the same as our open first string.

Track 77

Fourth String Study

50

Track 78

Accidentals on the 4th String: G♯/A♭ and A♯/B♭

G♯/A♭

■ To play the note G♯ (or its enharmonic equivalent, A♭), place your first finger at the first fret of the fourth string.

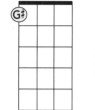

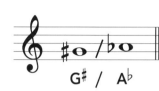

G♯ / A♭

A♯/B♭

■ To play the note A♯ (or its enharmonic equivalent, B♭), place your third finger at the third fret of the fourth string.

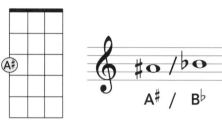

A♯ / B♭

Track 79

Happy Accidentals

Let's try some examples that include notes played on both the third and fourth strings.

Track 80

Ups & Downs

C & G String Boogie

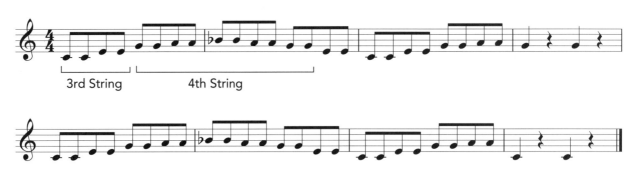

3rd String   4th String

We have now covered all the notes in the first position on the fourth string. For us to round out our knowledge of first and second positions, there is one more fourth-string note to cover at the fifth fret: C. This is the same pitch as the C we know on the first string, third fret. Remember that, when in second position, your first finger is at the second fret, and each finger covers the notes in succession up to the fifth fret.

C

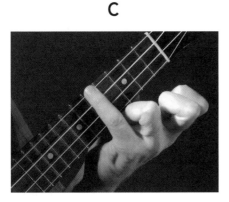

■ To play C, place your fourth finger at the fifth fret on the fourth string.

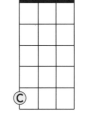

Try out the melody to "Go Tell Aunt Rhody" played entirely on the fourth string.

Go Tell Aunt Rhody (I've Got the Fourth String in My Head)

Lesson 13 | Common Stroke & Waltz Stroke

Track 84

The basic principle of strumming chords with the common stroke was covered in Lesson 2. When playing in a quarter-note (or downbeat) rhythm, we use downstrokes (⊓) with the thumb.

For eighth-note rhythms, we strum down (⊓) with the thumb on the beat and up (V) with the index finger on the "and" or upbeats.

Continue to work on this concept and master it.

Another version of the common stroke would be the ***index finger strum***. For this stroke, arch your index finger about halfway between fully curled into your hand and completely extended. Curl your other fingers into your palm, and use the tip of your index finger, positioning it roughly above the twelfth fret. Strum with your index finger on both the upstrokes and downstrokes. This is somewhat similar to using a pick.

The ***waltz stroke***, or how we strum in 3/4 time, can be done by strumming down with the thumb once and up twice with the index finger. This covers the three quarter-note beats and helps get a lilting waltz feel, while also giving the strum a little finesse.

Here are some new chords: A7, E7, D, and D7. Let's try them in some common and waltz stroke exercises and songs. Play them using both thumb and finger combinations as well as the index finger strum.

Track 85

New Chords: A7, E7, D, and D7

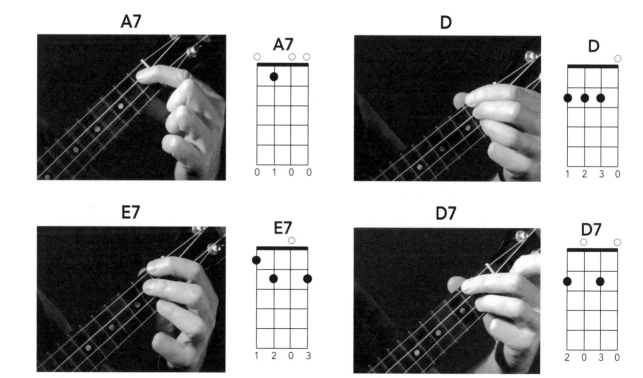

A7

D

E7

D7

First and Second Endings

The following exercises have a *first and second ending*, indicated by brackets with the numbers 1 and 2. When you reach the repeat sign in the first ending (:‖), go back to the beginning. On the second time through, skip the first ending and go on to the second ending.

Track 86

Common Stroke 1

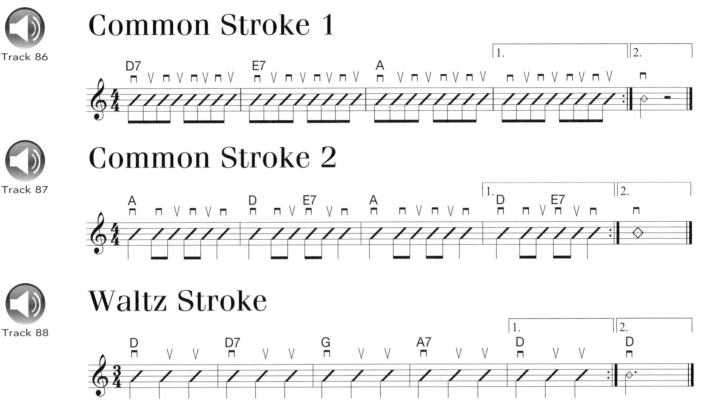

Track 87

Common Stroke 2

Track 88

Waltz Stroke

Play the chords to this next tune using the waltz stroke. You can also try picking out the melody.

Waltz Stroke Accompaniment

Track 89

My Bonnie Lies Over the Ocean

My Bon - nie lies o - ver the o - cean.___ My Bon - nie lies

o - ver the sea.___ My Bon - nie lies o - ver the o - cean.___ Oh,

bring back my Bon - nie to me.___ Bring back, oh, bring back, oh,

bring back my Bon - nie to me, to me. Bring back, oh,

bring back, oh, bring back my Bon - nie to me._____

Dotted Notes

As we know, a dot extends any note by one half its value.

| dotted quarter note (one and a half beats) | = | quarter note (one beat) | + | eighth note (one half of a beat) |

Strum this Hawaiian favorite using the given common stroke accompaniment, and then pick out the melody as well.

Common Stroke Accompaniment

Track 90

Aloha Oe

Ukulele History: Queen Liliuokalani

The last monarch of Hawaii was an avid musician and composer of over 150 songs, "Aloha Oe" being the most famous. She was a ukulele player and, like her brother, King Kalakuaua before her, did much to promote the popularity of the uke with the Hawaiian people. It was Queen Liliuokalani's claim that the name "ukulele" meant "the gift that came here," from the words "uku" (gift) and "lele" (to come).

Tablature

Track 91

Up to this point, we've learned and utilized standard music notation to play our exercises and melodies. This is very helpful in understanding music as a whole and in referencing a multitude of musical literary sources that may not necessarily be specific to the ukulele. However, there is another form of musical notation called **tablature**. This is a system of musical notation that's specific to an instrument. It has been used for hundreds of years, and, in fact, a substantial amount of early lute and keyboard manuscript was written in tablature.

Ukulele tablature consists of four lines on the tab staff, which represent the four strings of the uke. The top line represents the first string (A), the second line represents the second string (E), and so on.

Tablature is essentially a road map of the fretboard and tells you exactly where to play a note as you travel through a tune.

Reading Pitches

Numbers are placed on the lines to indicate at which fret a note is to be played. The number "0" is used for open strings.

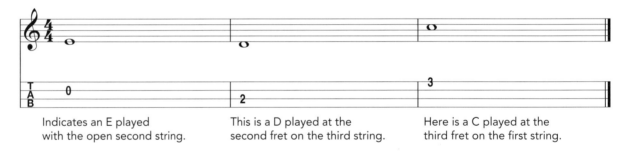

| Indicates an E played with the open second string. | This is a D played at the second fret on the third string. | Here is a C played at the third fret on the first string. |

Reading Rhythms

The tab staff is divided into measures, just like standard notation. When rhythm values are used in tab, they are indicated as follows. Rests and dotted note values appear as they do in standard notation.

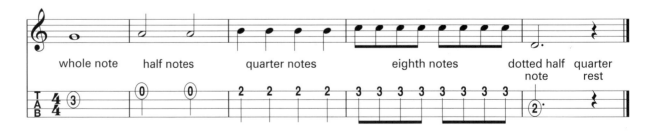

whole note   half notes   quarter notes   eighth notes   dotted half note   quarter rest

Pushing Boundaries

Track 92

Review of Movable Scales

In Lessons 9 and 10, we learned about movable major and minor scales. Let's take a moment to review the patterns and look at how we may use these concepts to help move us up the neck. This will open the door to melodies and chordal possibilities that we cannot achieve in first and second positions alone. In addition, we'll gain a greater understanding of the ukulele.

Here are our movable major and minor scale patterns:

▶ Circled note = root note. These patterns may be moved to any root/position on the neck to play the desired scale.

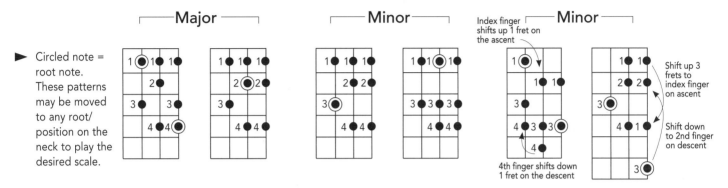

The first four of these scale patterns are in a box form, which means your fingers maintain one position. However, for us to play the complete minor scale (from root to its octave), we must shift positions within the patterns.

Let's apply these final patterns to an E minor scale to help illustrate how to make these shifts. This will bring us up to the fifth position. We've seen most of these notes, but in lower positions. Please refer to the tablature to familiarize yourself with their placement on the fingerboard in the higher positions. Before you play the scales, here are three notes in the fifth position we haven't seen thus far: high E♭, E, and F.

Track 93

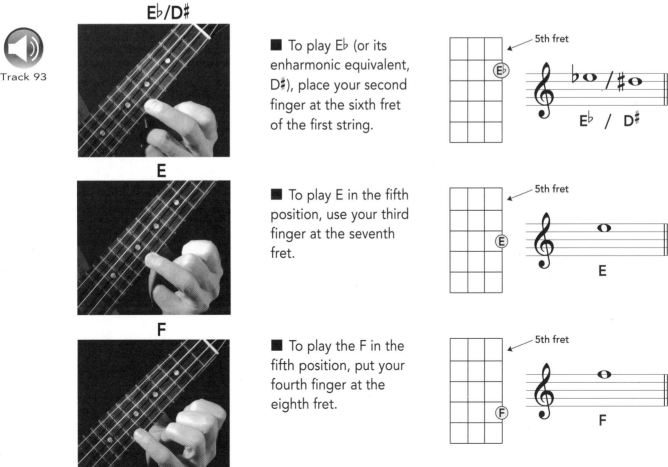

■ To play E♭ (or its enharmonic equivalent, D♯), place your second finger at the sixth fret of the first string.

■ To play E in the fifth position, use your third finger at the seventh fret.

■ To play the F in the fifth position, put your fourth finger at the eighth fret.

Track 94

E Minor Scale 1

This pattern includes a shift between adjacent strings.

E Minor Scale 2

This pattern includes a shift on a single string.

Now, let's put these concepts to use and play some tunes. Starting in the fifth position, we'll play a couple of holiday numbers, employing both major and minor keys.

"Joy to the World" is a popular Christmas melody that utilizes all the notes of the major scale. We'll be playing it in the key of F major, with the root on the third string at the fifth fret.

Track 95

Joy to the World

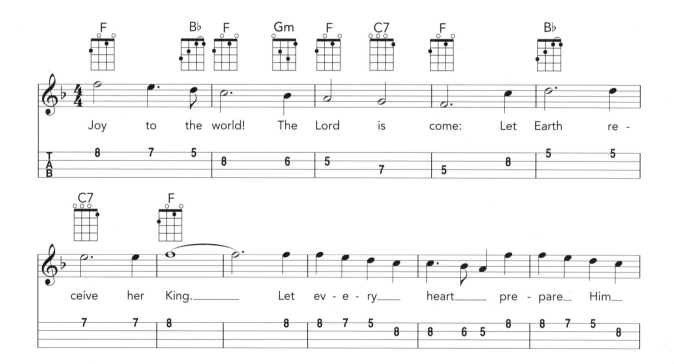

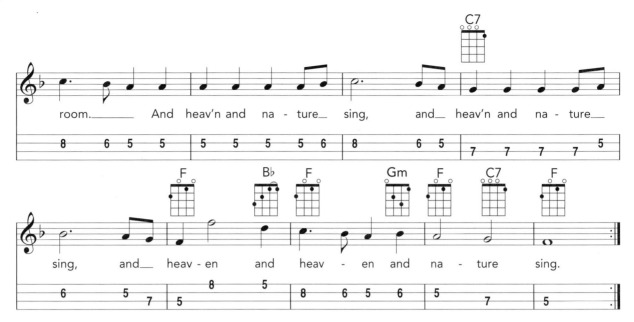

Next, we'll play "We Three Kings of Orient Are." This piece starts in G minor, with the root on the third string at the seventh fret. It concludes in B♭ major, with the root on the second string at the sixth fret.

We Three Kings of Orient Are

Now, let's go to the seventh position to try a couple of classic traditional melodies: "Shady Grove" and "Miss MacLeod's Reel," in A minor and G major, respectively. We have two unfamiliar notes in this position: F♯ and G.

F♯

Track 97

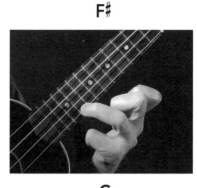

■ To play high F♯ in the seventh position (or its enharmonic equivalent, G♭), place your third finger at the ninth fret of the first string.

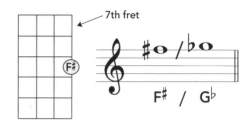

G

■ To play high G in the seventh position, place your fourth finger at the tenth fret of the first string.

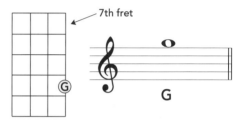

As previously mentioned, use the tablature to help familiarize yourself with the new locations of notes in this higher position.

After you learn the melody, strum the chords and sing along.

Shady Grove

Track 98

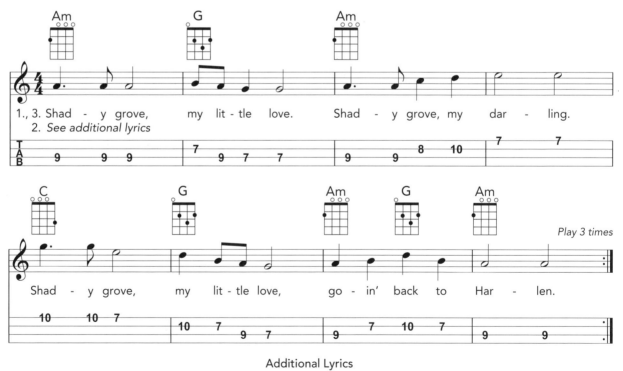

Additional Lyrics

2. Peaches in the summertime,
Apples in the fall.
If I don't find the gal I love,
I don't want none at all.

Miss MacLeod's Reel

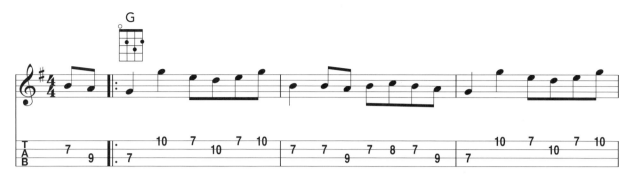

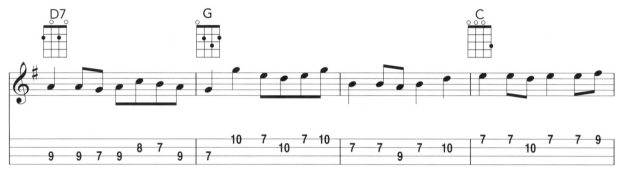

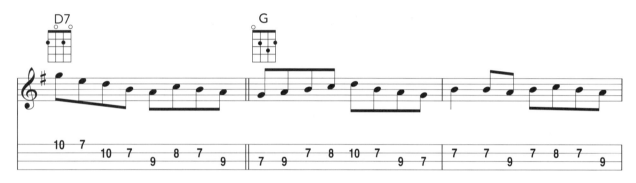

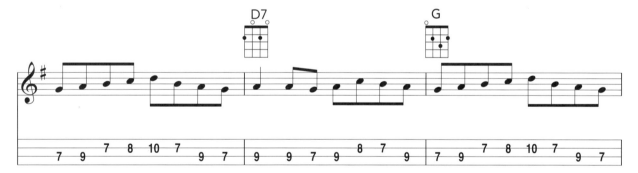

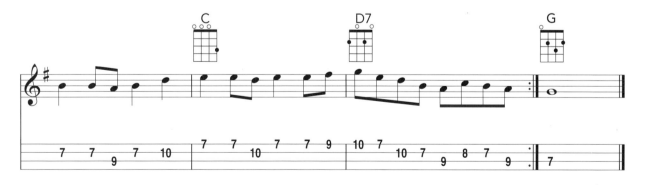

Track 100

This next piece requires a momentary shift from the seventh to the tenth position (to reach the high A). Also, we have some new notes: G#/A♭ and high A.

G#/A♭

■ To play G# (or its enharmonic equivalent, A♭) in the tenth position, place your second finger at the eleventh fret on the first string.

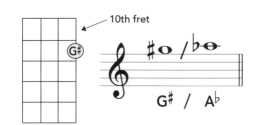

A

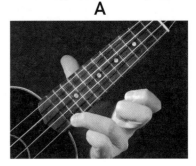

■ To play high A, place your third finger at the twelfth fret on the first string.

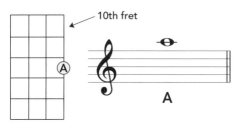

Track 101

God Rest Ye Merry, Gentlemen

Now you should know all the notes up to the twelfth fret, in one position or another. Keep in mind that position playing is a valuable tool at your disposal—not a rule that can't be broken. You should feel free to arrange and play melodies in whatever way works best for you.

Movable Chord Shapes

Track 102

The easiest and most efficient way to expand our chord vocabulary is through the use of *movable chord shapes*. A movable chord shape is simply a chord with no open strings. These shapes can be used anywhere on the neck, giving you as many as a dozen different chords. All of these shapes stem from our open chords, but our fingerings usually require some repositioning to accommodate the first finger barring over, or at least covering, any fret that would have been previously open.

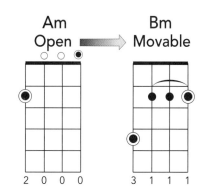

Am Open ⟹ Bm Movable

2 0 0 0   3 1 1 1

◉ = root

Major

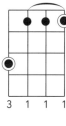

3 2 1 1

2 3 4 1

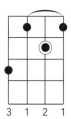

3 1 2 1

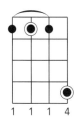

1 1 1 4

Minor

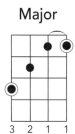

3 1 1 1

3 4 2 1

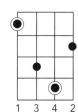

1 3 4 2

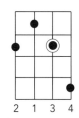

2 1 3 4

Dominant 7

1 2 1 1

2 3 1 4

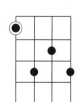

1 3 2 4

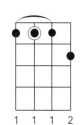

1 1 1 2

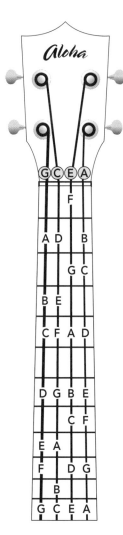

Lesson 17 | Hammer-Ons, Pull-Offs & Slides

Track 103

Hammer-ons, *pull-offs*, and *slides* are invaluable left-hand techniques. When employed, you cause two or more notes to sound by only picking the string once.

Hammer-Ons

To execute a *hammer-on*, you pick the first note (open or fretted) and then decisively (but rhythmically in time) bring the tip of the appropriate finger down at the fret of the second (higher) note on the same string. When sufficient force is used, this causes the second note to sound without having to be picked.

The *hammer-on* is indicated by a *slur* from a lower note to a higher note. The *slur* is a curved line in music that looks identical to a tie, except it connects different pitches together, indicating a *legato* feel. *Legato* is a musical term that means smooth and connected, without breaks between the successive tones.

Track 104

Hammer-On from an Open String

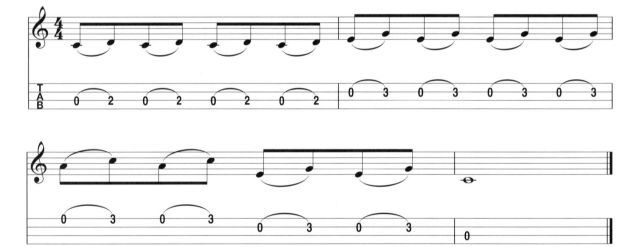

Hammer-On from a Fretted Note

Track 105

64

Pull-Offs

In order to perform a ***pull-off***, sound the fretted higher note with your picking hand, then pull off the finger fretting that note in a slightly downward motion, so it actually plucks (and sounds) the fretted or open lower note below it.

The pull-off is indicated by a slur from a higher note to a lower one.

Pull-Off to an Open String

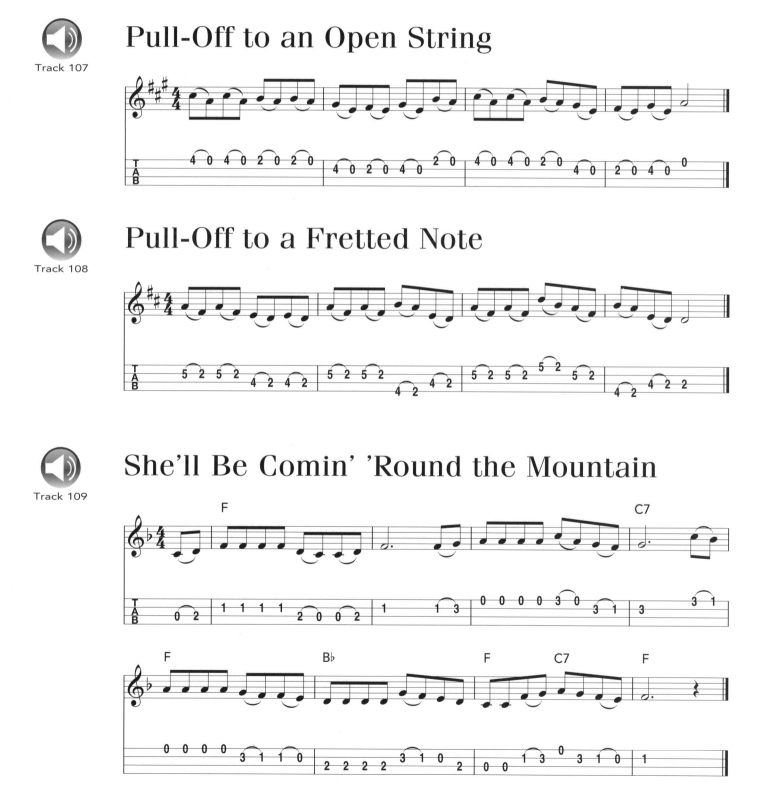

Pull-Off to a Fretted Note

She'll Be Comin' 'Round the Mountain

Play the melody of this next tune that features hammer-ons and pull-offs. When playing the chords for this song, try out some of our movable forms in the second section.

Jack of Diamonds

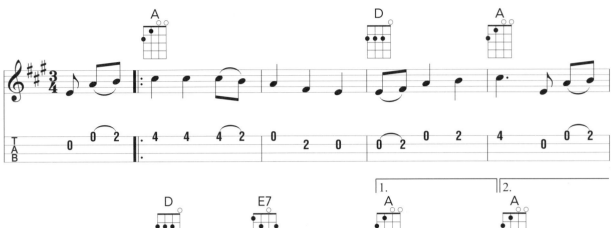

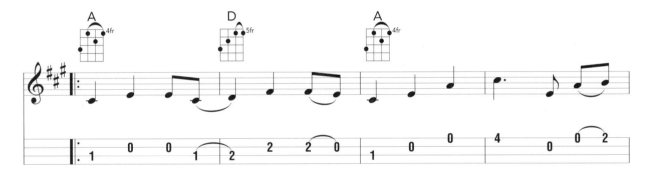

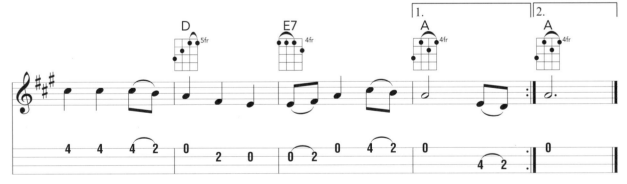

Slides

To execute a *slide*, you pick a fretted note and, while maintaining pressure, move (or slide) your finger up or down the fretboard to the desired second note.

The slide is indicated by a straight line positioned at an upward or downward angle between two notes.

The second note, or destination note, can be picked or not picked. If the second note is not to be picked, a slur also connects the two notes. Sometimes slides are used as embellishments, not necessarily tying two notes together. In this case, you begin the slide at an arbitrary point (usually lower), with no real rhythmic or tonal value, and then slide into the target pitch. These types of slides are notated with a sloped line before or after a single pitch.

Slide Up

Slide Up, Down & Around

Sourwood Mountain

Lesson 18 | Time Marches On

Track 115

Up to this point, we've played songs in both 4/4 (common time) and 3/4 (waltz time). These meters are part of a group called **simple time signatures**. There are a good many other ways that a beat can be laid down for a tune. We'll now explore a couple of these other meters.

Cut Time

Cut time, usually indicated on the staff by (¢), is 2/2 time signature. This means there are two beats per measure, and the half note gets the beat. This meter, also known as "alla breve," has an accelerated and driving feel and is a common time signature for marches.

> **Alla breve** is Italian for "Alla" (according to the) + "Breve" (twice as fast as normal).

A New Road Map

D.S. al Fine, or *dal segno al fine*, literally means "[play] from the sign to the end." This is an indication to start back at the *segno* (𝄋) and continue playing until you reach the word "fine."

D.C. al Fine, or *da capo al fine*, means "from the head [beginning] to the end." This is an indication to repeat back to the beginning of the music and continue until you reach the word "fine."

Let's try playing this familiar march to get the feel of cut time. To play an accompaniment strum, two solid downstrokes work well for a downbeat emphasis.

Cut Time Accompaniment

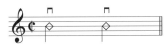

Marine's Hymn

Track 116

Introducing 16th Notes

If you divide an eighth note in half, you get a sixteenth note. A sixteenth note looks like an eighth note, but it has two flags on its stem instead of one: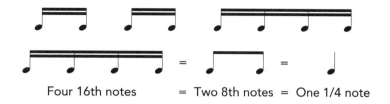

Consecutive sixteenth notes are connected with a double beam:

Four 16th notes = Two 8th notes = One 1/4 note

If we count the quarter note beat while tapping our foot and eighth notes by putting "and" between the beats, we can count sixteenth notes by adding the syllables "e" and "a" between the eighth notes: "1-e-and-a."

1   2   3   &   4   &   1   e   &   a   2   &   a   3   &   4

A sixteenth rest is counted in the same manner.

1   2   &   3   e   &   a   4   &   1   &   a   2   e   &   a   3   &   4

2/4 Time

Sixteenth notes are a common rhythmic figure in 2/4 time. In 2/4 time, the quarter note gets the beat, and there are two beats per measure. This time signature is commonly used for polkas, fiddle tunes, and many other traditional or folk melodies.

Unlike 2/2, where a very straight ahead downbeat approach works well, 2/4 either accents the second beat and/or the "and" of both beats. Here's an example.

Now we come to another stroke that can be very effective in 2/4 time...

The Pick Stroke

With the *pick stroke*, we pick a single note with our thumb on the downbeat (usually on strings three or four) and strum up with the index finger on the upbeat, or the "and."

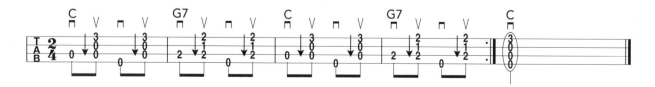

Time to get out the dancin' shoes and play a 2/4 tune! The melody is written on the top staff and the accompaniment chord pattern is shown on the tablature staff below. Be sure to try out both parts.

Oh, Them Golden Slippers

Track 118

► Keep thumb alternating between the third and fourth strings throughout.

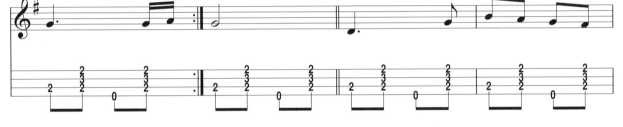

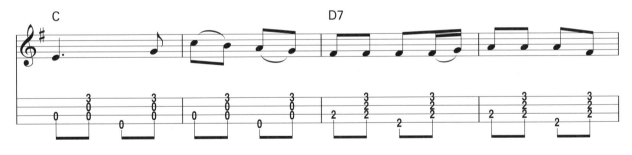

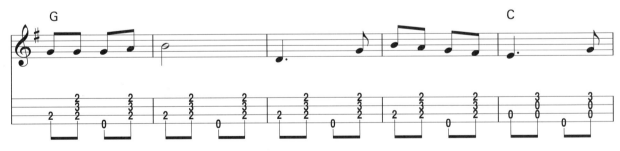

Time & Time Again

Track 119

Compound Time

Compound time signatures have a beat that is subdivided by three. Some typical compound time signatures are 6/8, 9/8, and 12/8. For example, 6/8 time indicates that we count six eighth notes per measure, or two groups of three.

Triplets

Triplets are units of three eighth notes played in the space of one beat. In compound time signatures, the foot taps in the space of a dotted quarter note. We subdivide those dotted quarter notes into three eighth notes, counted with emphasis on the first note of the set: **1**-2-3, **2**-2-3, etc. You may also get the proper rhythm by saying "tri-puh-let, tri-puh-let," or "1-and-uh, 2-and-uh," etc.

Triplets also occur in simple time signatures, though not as frequently, and may be counted in much the same way. In 4/4, start with the quarter-note beat, counting 1, 2, 3, 4:

Then divide that into even eighth-note divisions: 1 & 2 & 3 & 4 &:

Now, if we squeeze an extra eighth note evenly into the same space as these two, we get a triplet: **1** 2 3, **2** 2 3, **3** 2 3, **4** 2 3:

Triplets in simple time signatures are always notated with a "3" at the beam to indicate there are three notes in the space of two.

Play the familiar melody below in 6/8 time, then strum the chords using this accompaniment pattern:

6/8 Time Accompaniment

Track 120

Hickory Dickory Dock

Triplet Stroke

To strum a *triplet stroke*, we:

1. Strum down (⊓) with the
   index finger.

2. Follow with a downstroke (⊓)
   of the thumb.

3. Then, strum up (∨) with the
   index finger.

To get the feel of this and other strokes, it can be helpful to mute the strings with your fret hand to create a percussive (drum beat) sound while you strum. Just lightly touch the strings with your fret hand without pushing them down to the fretboard. This method enables you to hear the accuracy of your rhythms a little more clearly. You can also use this technique to occasionally add a rhythmic spice to your playing.

Track 122

Triplet Exercise 1

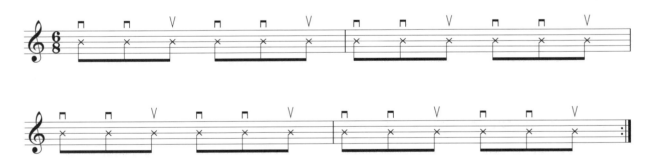

Sometimes the syllables of words can help you learn a rhythm.

Track 123

Triplet Exercise 2

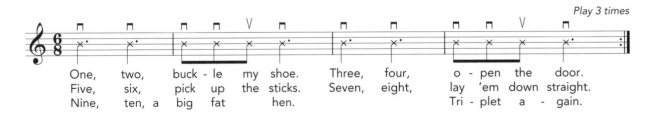

Now here's a fun triplet tune in 4/4 time that includes the triplet stroke and the muted-string technique.

Triplet Your Uke
(When You're Happy and You Know It)

New Chords: F7 and B♭m

(From our movable-form arsenal)

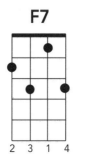

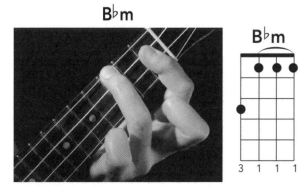

Here, we'll strum triplets in 12/8 time, which is often referred to as "doo wop" time. It's used for many songs from the '50s, as well as slow blues.

Da Uke Doo Wop

First play the chords with a triplet stroke, then pluck the melody to this timeless classic.

Triplet Stroke Accompaniment

When Johnny Comes Marching Home

When John - ny comes march - ing home a - gain, hur - rah!_____ Hur - rah!_____ We'll

give him a heart - y wel - come then, hur - rah!_____ Hur - rah!_____ The

men will cheer and the boys will shout. The la - dies they___ will all turn out and we'll

all feel gay when John - ny comes march - ing home.

The Shuffle Stroke

The **shuffle stroke** is similar to the common stroke, generally used in 4/4 time, and associated with boogie-woogie blues and jazz. It also works well in compound and other meters. You've already heard an example of the shuffle used on the song "Triplet Your Uke" on page 73. Eighth notes are played unevenly or "swung"—the first note played long and the second note short. This is timed as if you were playing a triplet with the first two notes tied together:

The pulse is also accented more heavily on the second and fourth beats, as opposed to the first and third. There is an extra dash of spice, which can be thrown into a shuffle to really add some "boogie" to its "woogie," by switching on and off between a chord tone and an additional note (usually a whole step above) on every other beat. This creates a pendulum-like, rocking back-and-forth feel. This "boogie beat" concept was put into play by early barrelhouse pianists and has been carried on through blues and rock and roll.

Shuffle Boogie

▶ In this case, we add a D note on the third string to both chords every second and fourth beat.

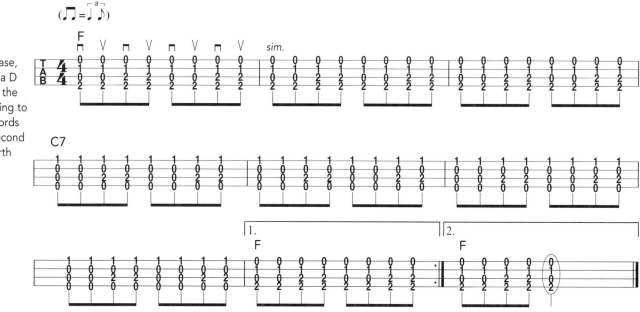

This handy progression could be used to fit many songs, such as "Polly Wolly Doodle," "Iko, Iko," and the ukulele classic, "It Ain't Gonna Rain No Mo'."

Ukulele History: Wendell Hall

Known as the "red-headed music maker," Wendell Hall was an early star of the ukulele on the vaudeville stage, radio, and on record. His 1923 recording of "It Ain't Gonna Rain No Mo'" was a multi-million seller and spent six weeks at number one on the U.S. charts.

New Chords: C6 and D♭6

Track 130 · Track 131

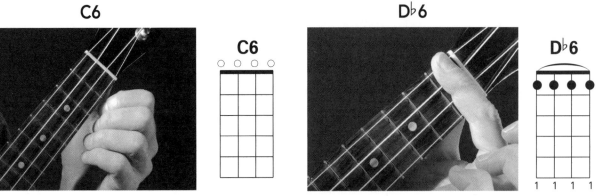

In this classic blues song, we'll demonstrate how effective it can be to vary the rhythms by switching up our strokes. Centering on a shuffle, adding triplets and straight quarter-note downstrokes at key points gives this 12-bar blues the depth it deserves.

See See Rider

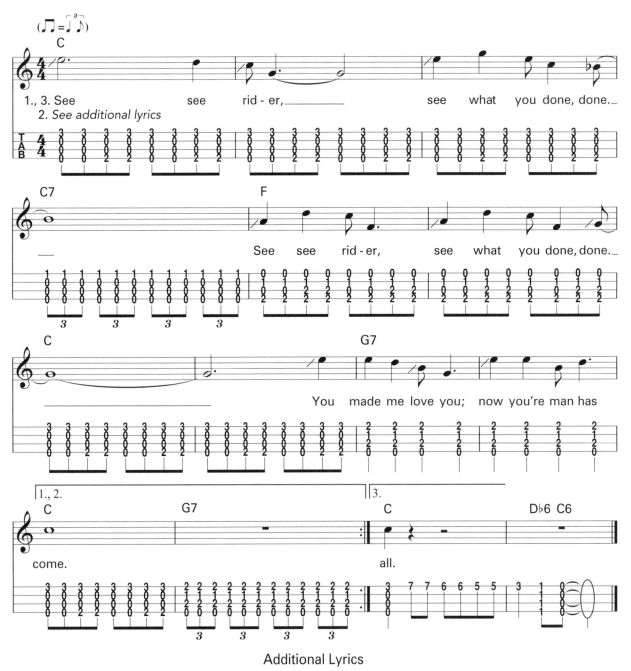

Additional Lyrics

2. I'm goin' away, baby, won't be back till fall.
Goin' away, baby, won't be back till fall.
If I find a good gal, I won't be back at all.

76

Fingerpicking

Track 132

Fingerpicking on the ukulele can encompass essentially all melodic and harmonic playing that is approached without the use of a pick. Historically, most ukulele playing has been done with the fingerstyle technique.

Picking with the fingers offers a great many options for voicings and textures on the ukulele—things that would be difficult, if not impossible, with the sole use of the pick. Let's take a look at some specifics.

As we learned in Lesson 1, the fingers on the fret hand are numbered from index to pinky: 1, 2, 3, and 4. The fingers on the picking hand have their own designations. These letters are abbreviations from the internationally known system of Spanish words and letters:

p	pulgar	=	thumb
i	indice	=	index finger
m	medio	=	middle finger
a	anular	=	ring finger

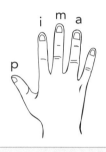

Arpeggios

Arpeggios, or broken chords, are a huge part of fingerpicking, both for song accompaniment and for instrumental solos. This means that we play the notes in a chord individually (often in succession), as opposed to strumming, where they are played all at once. There are many different picking patterns and combinations available, so experiment with as many as you can discover.

Let's try a few arpeggios…

Track 133

Arpeggio 1

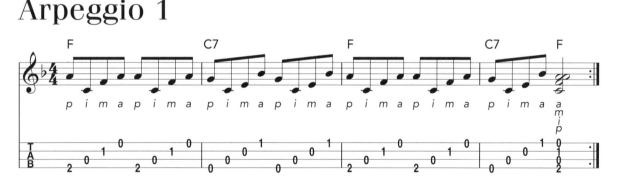

Track 134

Arpeggio 2

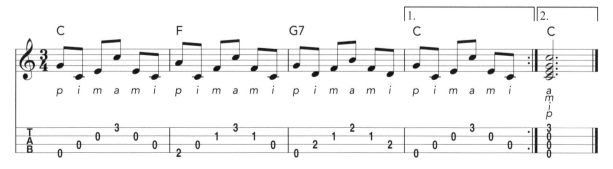

Alternate Thumb 1

▶ Keep your thumb switching between the third and fourth strings.

Alternate Thumb 2

P.M. Lullaby

Picking Blues

Here's a classic fingerpicking tune in 6/8 time.

House of the Rising Sun

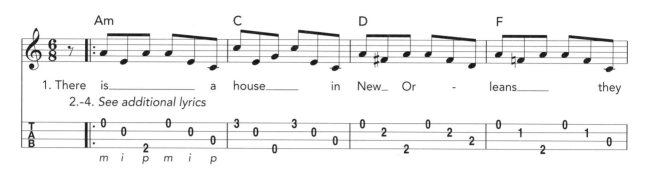

1. There is _____ a house _____ in New_ Or - leans _____ they

2.-4. *See additional lyrics*

m i p m i p

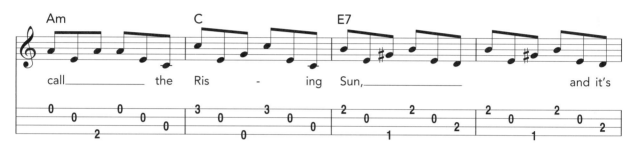

call _____ the Ris - ing Sun, _____ and it's

been _____ the ruin _____ of man-y a poor boy, and

God, _____ I know _____ I'm one. _____

Additional Lyrics

2. If I had listened to what mama said,
   I'd 'a' been at home today.
   Being so young and foolish, poor girl,
   Let a gambler lead me astray.

3. My mother, she's a tailor,
   She sews my new blue jeans.
   My sweetheart's a drunkard, Lord,
   Drinks down in New Orleans.

4. The only thing a drunkard needs
   Is a suitcase and a trunk.
   The only time he's ever satisfied
   Is when he's on a drunk.

Playing Two Parts at Once

Track 140

We have now learned many different types of melodies and a variety of ways in which we may accompany them with chords. Now, let's take a look at some new ways to fill out our playing by adding harmonies to melodies and melodic elements to chords.

Parallel 3rds & 6ths

One very effective way to harmonize a melody is with the use of **parallel 3rds** and/or **6ths**. For example, if we take a melody note and stack a **3rd** on top of it, we create a harmony, or two parts played simultaneously.

What do we mean by **3rds**? Well, we need to look at a major scale to find the answer. Here is a C major scale (but any scale can work). If we number each note of the scale 1–8:

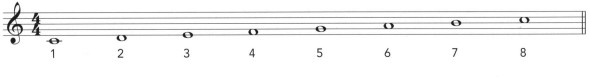

…with C, the root, being "1," then E would fall on "3," which makes it the 3rd. Play these two notes together, and we have the harmony of a 3rd.

3rd

We can continue this all the way up the scale, effectively harmonizing each note with the successive 3rd above. A 3rd above D is F, a 3rd above E is G, and so on. Visually, this can be observed in the written music by "stacking" the note in the next space or the next line. Some 3rds are major (two whole steps apart), some are minor (a whole and a half step apart):

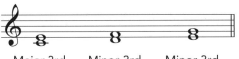

Major 3rd   Minor 3rd   Minor 3rd

Basic chords (or **triads**) are constructed by stacking a 3rd on top of a 3rd.

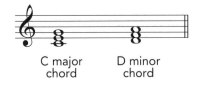

C major   D minor
chord   chord

Now, it's time to play through a few scale combinations, harmonizing with parallel 3rds. Pick these notes with individual fingers, or by "pinching" between the thumb and a finger.

Here's a C major scale harmonized in 3rds on the second and third strings.

Track 141

C Major – Parallel 3rds

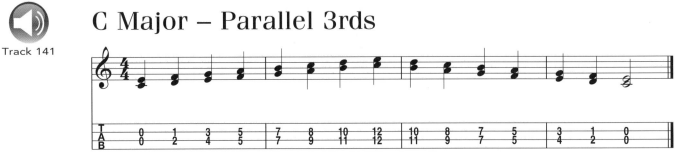

Here we have an F major scale harmonized in 3rds on the first and second strings.

Track 142

F Major – Parallel 3rds

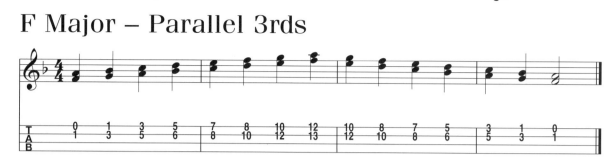

If we reverse the order of these note pairings—let's say C and E—with C being the higher of the two, then it becomes a 6th, because E is six notes below C. The sound of 6ths is used in many types of music, from Hawaiian to blues and swing, just to name a few.

Here are some scale exercises demonstrating parallel 6ths.

Track 143

C Major – Parallel 6ths

Track 144

A Major – Parallel 6ths

Now check out this Hawaiian waltz featuring both parallel 3rds and 6ths.

Track 145

Isle of My Love

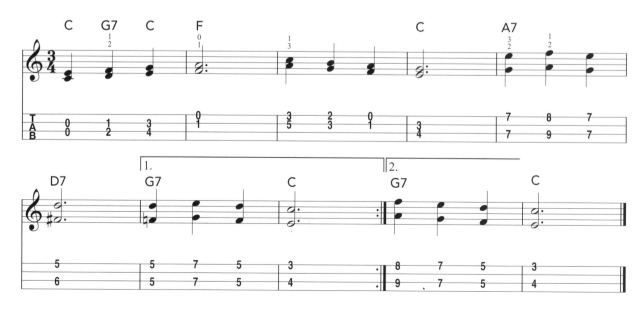

The Dotted Eighth Note

The next tune includes this new rhythm, the *dotted eighth note*.

$$\text{dotted eighth note} \quad = \quad \text{eighth note} \quad + \quad \text{sixteenth note}$$

Dotted eighth notes are sometimes beamed together with sixteenth notes to create this rhythm:

Battle Hymn of the Republic

The first part of this piece incorporates a "pinch" between the thumb and middle finger on the fourth and second strings, alternating with the index finger playing the upbeats on the third string. The second part has the index and middle playing together on the downbeat, while the thumb plays the upbeat.

Andantino

Track 147

Chord Melody

In the following arrangements, we use a **sweep stroke**. To accomplish this, we sweep down through a chord with the thumb until we arrive at the desired melody note and give it a little more emphasis. Employing this technique as we pick through a melody enables us to play both chords and melodies simultaneously.

Skip to My Lou

Track 148

Bingo

Track 149

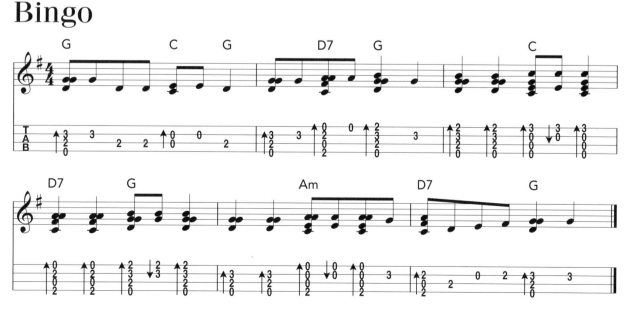

New Chords: E6, A6, and D6

This is an easy, movable chord form for which we barre straight across all four strings.

The root note is found on the third string, so D6 is a full barre at the second fret, E6 is at the fourth fret, and A6 is at the ninth fret. This is the same form we've encountered previously as a D♭6.

Here are two more tunes arranged for chord-melody uke. "Corrina" includes the new barre chords as well as the "pinch" technique. The strum arrows in the tablature staff tell you where to use the sweep stroke to emphasize the melody notes.

Track 151

Corrina

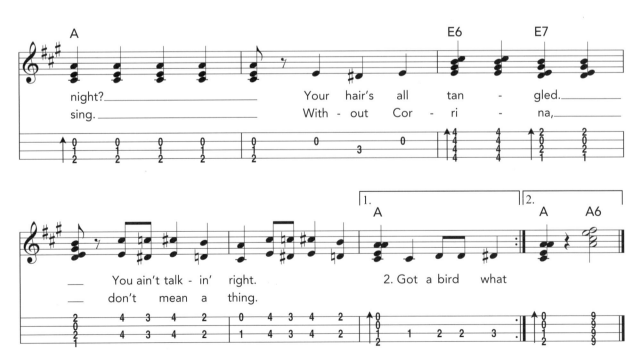

Danny Boy

Tremolo & the Roll Stroke

Track 153

Tremolo

Given that notes on the ukulele quickly fade away after being picked, we must address how to create long, sustained tones, similar to that produced by wind and bowed instruments. For this to be achieved, we must use a technique called *tremolo*.

To play the tremolo stroke:

- Fold the second, third, and fourth fingers of your picking hand into your palm.

- For a focused tremolo, encompassing one or two strings, use only your index finger in rapid downstrokes and upstrokes. This movement stems largely from the main and second knuckles of the index finger, akin to a scratching motion.

- For a wider tremolo (strumming three to four strings), more wrist movement is required. Use of the nail yields a louder, more percussive sound.

This should be as quick and constant as possible, creating a flickering, beautiful shimmering effect. The next tune features this new technique (shown in the notation with slash marks:), as well as the new Fm chord.

New Chord: Fm

Fm

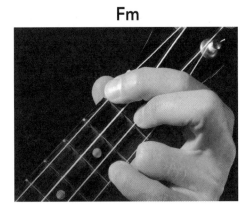

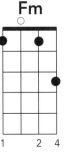

Track 154

Cielito Lindo (My Pretty Darling)

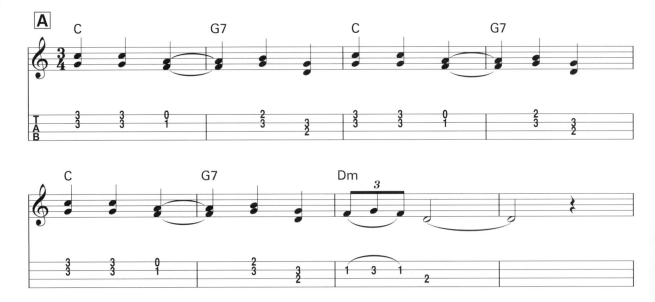

Track 155

The Roll Stroke

To play the (five finger) *roll stroke*, begin with your fingers curled into the palm of your picking hand. Fan your fingers out one by one across all of the strings in a continuous downward motion. Start with the pinky (fourth) finger, followed by the ring, middle, index fingers, and finish with the thumb, completing the roll stroke.

This next song, "Habenera" (from Bizet's *Carmen*), is a very cool Spanish-flavored piece. It works great to accompany this with all quarter-note downstrokes, adding the roll stroke on the third beat of every measure.

There's also a new, easy chord for this song: G6.

New Chord: G6

G6

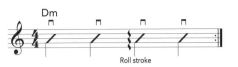

First play through the melody of this next tune, then try out the chord accompaniment with the roll stroke.

Track 156

Roll Stroke Accompaniment

Track 157

Habenera

Chord Glossary

These are chords you will find in many popular songs. You don't have to buy music that is written specifically for the ukulele—just make sure the music has chord symbols.

A good way to learn new songs and chords at the same time is to draw ukulele chord diagrams directly above the chord symbols on the music. You'll be surprised by how quickly you learn new chords when you copy the diagrams this way.

Major Chords

A
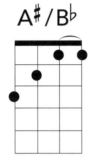

A♯/B♭
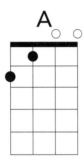

B
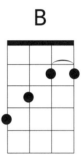

C
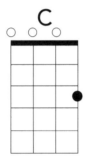

C♯/D♭

D
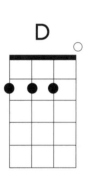

D♯/E♭
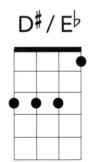

E
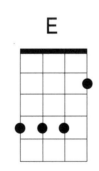

F
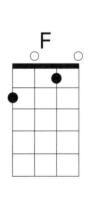

F♯/G♭
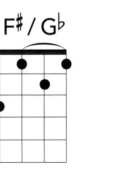

G
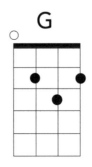

G♯/A♭
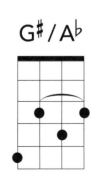

Minor Chords

Am
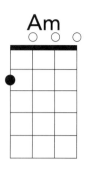

A#m/B♭m
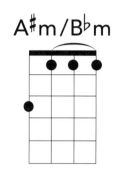

Bm
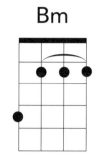

Cm
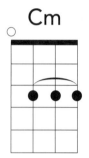

C#m/D♭m
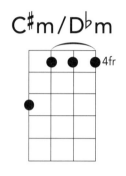

Dm
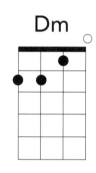

D#m/E♭m
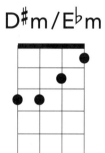

Em
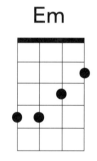

Fm

F#m/G♭m
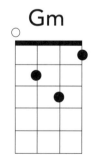

Gm
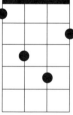

G#m/A♭m

Dominant Chords

A7

A#7/B♭7
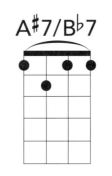

B7

C7

C#7/D♭7

D7

D#7/E♭7
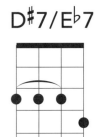

E7
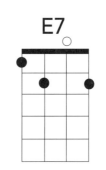

F7

F#7/G♭7
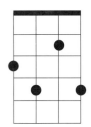

G7

G#7/A♭7
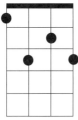

Miscellaneous Moveable Chord Forms

Circled note = root

C6
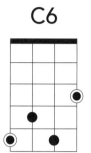

D6
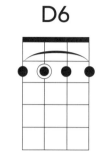

A°7 E♭°7 F#°7 C°7

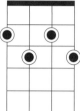

A♭°7 D°7 F°7 B°7
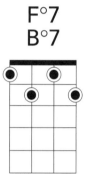

Cmaj7

Dmaj7

Cm7
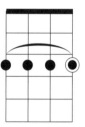

Dm7
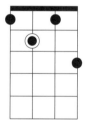

Dm7♭5
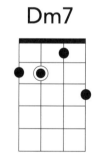

Am7♭5
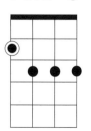

D+

B♭+
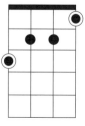

How to Change a String

Strings need to be changed when they break, or when they get old and go "dead" in tone. It's easiest to remove and replace one string at a time. Make sure to replace with the same gauge of each string. Wrap one end of the new string through the bridge hole as shown in the diagram and pull it tight. Then feed the other end through the tuning peg hole, making sure the string sits in the nut slot and is not hung up on the edge of the fingerboard. Leave about a half inch of slack, to allow the string to wrap around the tuning post about three times when tightened. Hold it in place with one hand while tightening until it stays by itself. Trim off the excess string at the top and bottom with a pair of wire cutters, and then tune the string up to pitch.

1. Insert string through bridge hole from the top.

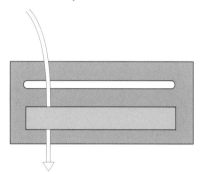

2. Wrap over block, under string, through loop.

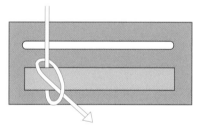

3. Wrap until last winding is near bottom hole.

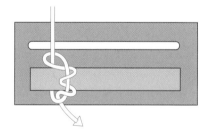

4. Pull to tighten.

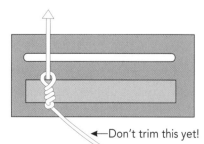

←Don't trim this yet!

5. Insert string into peg from the inside of the headstock.

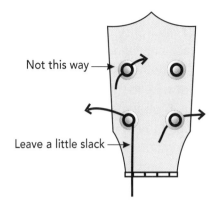

Not this way

Leave a little slack

6. Pinch the string on the peg for several turns to keep the string from slipping.

7. Turn tuning key with your other hand. Make sure the string wraps neatly down the peg. Tune string to pitch and make sure it isn't slipping.

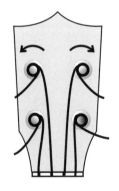

8. Trim off excess string at both ends of the ukulele, but leave about 1/4".

New strings will go through a stretching period before they stay in tune. You can tug on them a little bit to speed up the process. Tune up regularly as you play. If you are sure you have the strings installed correctly and the ukulele still won't stay in tune, you may have loose tuning pegs. Most guitar shops can fix this and other problems.

Play Today! Series

The Ultimate Self-Teaching Series

These are complete guides to the basics, designed to offer quality instruction, terrific songs, and professional-quality audio with tons of full-demo tracks and instruction. Each book includes over 70 great songs and examples!

Play Accordion Today!
00701744 Level 1 Book/Audio $10.99
00702657 Level 1 Songbook Book/Audio $12.99

Play Alto Sax Today!
00842049 Level 1 Book/Audio $9.99
00842050 Level 2 Book/Audio $9.99
00320359 DVD $14.95
00842051 Songbook Book/Audio $12.95
00699555 Beginner's – Level 1
              Book/Audio & DVD $19.95
00699492 Play Today Plus Book/Audio ... $14.95

Play Banjo Today!
00699897 Level 1 Book/Audio $9.99
00701006 Level 2 Book/Audio $9.99
00320913 DVD $14.99
00115999 Songbook Book/Audio $12.99
00701873 Beginner's – Level 1
              Book/Audio & DVD $19.95

Play Bass Today!
00842020 Level 1 Book/Audio $9.99
00842036 Level 2 Book/Audio $9.99
00320356 DVD $14.95
00842037 Songbook Book/Audio $12.95
00699552 Beginner's – Level 1
              Book/Audio & DVD $19.99

Play Cello Today!
00151353 Level 1 Book/Audio $9.99

Play Clarinet Today!
00842046 Level 1 Book/Audio $9.99
00842047 Level 2 Book/Audio $9.99
00320358 DVD $14.95
00842048 Songbook Book/Audio $12.95
00699554 Beginner's – Level 1
              Book/Audio & DVD $19.95
00699490 Play Today Plus Book/Audio ... $14.95

Play Dobro Today!
00701505 Level 1 Book/Audio $9.99

Play Drums Today!
00842021 Level 1 Book/Audio $9.99
00842038 Level 2 Book/Audio $9.95
00320355 DVD $14.95
00842039 Songbook Book/Audio $12.95
00699551 Beginner's – Level 1
              Book/Audio & DVD $19.95
00703291 Starter $24.99

Play Flute Today
00842043 Level 1 Book/Audio $9.95
00842044 Level 2 Book/Audio $9.99
00320360 DVD $14.95
00842045 Songbook Book/Audio $12.95
00699553 Beginner's – Level 1
              Book/Audio & DVD $19.95

Play Guitar Today!
00696100 Level 1 Book/Audio $9.99
00696101 Level 2 Book/Audio $9.99
00320353 DVD $14.95
00696102 Songbook Book/Audio $12.99
00699544 Beginner's – Level 1
              Book/Audio & DVD $19.95
00702431 Worship Songbook
              Book/Audio $12.99
00695662 Complete Kit $29.95

Play Harmonica Today!
00700179 Level 1 Book/Audio $9.99
00320653 DVD $14.99
00701875 Beginner's –
              Level 1 Book/Audio & DVD $19.95

Play Mandolin Today!
00699911 Level 1 Book/Audio $9.99
00320909 DVD $14.99
00115029 Songbook Book/Audio $12.99
00701874 Beginner's – Level 1
              Book/Audio & DVD $19.99

Play Piano Today!
00842019 Level 1 Book/Audio $9.99
00842040 Level 2 Book/Audio $9.95
00842041 Songbook Book/Audio $12.95
00699545 Beginner's – Level 1
              Book/Audio & DVD $19.95
00702415 Worship Songbook
              Book/Audio $12.99
00703707 Complete Kit $22.99

Play Recorder Today!
00700919 Level 1 Book/Audio $7.99
00119830 Complete Kit $19.99

Sing Today!
00699761 Level 1 Book/Audio $10.99

Play Trombone Today!
00699917 Level 1 Book/Audio $12.99
00320508 DVD $14.95

Play Trumpet Today!
00842052 Level 1 Book/Audio $9.99
00842053 Level 2 Book/Audio $9.95
00320357 DVD $14.95
00842054 Songbook Book/Audio $12.95
00699556 Beginner's – Level 1
              Book/Audio & DVD $19.95

Play Ukulele Today!
00699638 Level 1 Book/Audio $10.99
00699655 Play Today Plus Book/Audio $9.99
00320985 DVD $14.99
00701872 Beginner's – Level 1
              Book/Audio & DVD $19.95
00650743 Book/Audio/DVD with Ukulele $39.99
00701002 Level 2 Book/Audio $9.99
00702484 Level 2 Songbook Book/Audio $12.99
00703290 Starter $24.99

Play Viola Today!
00142679 Level 1 Book/Audio $9.99

Play Violin Today!
00699748 Level 1 Book/Audio $9.99
00701320 Level 2 Book/Audio $9.99
00321076 DVD $14.99
00701700 Songbook Book/Audio $12.99
00701876 Beginner's – Level 1
              Book/Audio & DVD $19.95

HAL•LEONARD®

www.halleonard.com

HAL•LEONARD® UKULELE PLAY-ALONG

AUDIO ACCESS INCLUDED

Now you can play your favorite songs on your uke with great-sounding backing tracks to help you sound like a bona fide pro! The audio also features playback tools so you can adjust the tempo without changing the pitch and loop challenging parts.

1. POP HITS
00701451 Book/CD Pack...............$15.99

2. UKE CLASSICS
00701452 Book/CD Pack...............$15.99

3. HAWAIIAN FAVORITES
00701453 Book/Online Audio..........$14.99

4. CHILDREN'S SONGS
00701454 Book/Online Audio..........$14.99

5. CHRISTMAS SONGS
00701696 Book/CD Pack...............$12.99

6. LENNON & McCARTNEY
00701723 Book/Online Audio..........$12.99

7. DISNEY FAVORITES
00701724 Book/Online Audio..........$12.99

8. CHART HITS
00701745 Book/CD Pack...............$15.99

9. THE SOUND OF MUSIC
00701784 Book/CD Pack...............$14.99

10. MOTOWN
00701964 Book/CD Pack...............$12.99

11. CHRISTMAS STRUMMING
00702458 Book/Online Audio..........$12.99

12. BLUEGRASS FAVORITES
00702584 Book/CD Pack...............$12.99

13. UKULELE SONGS
00702599 Book/CD Pack...............$12.99

14. JOHNNY CASH
00702615 Book/CD Pack...............$15.99

Prices, contents, and availability
subject to change without notice.

15. COUNTRY CLASSICS
00702834 Book/CD Pack...............$12.99

16. STANDARDS
00702835 Book/CD Pack...............$12.99

17. POP STANDARDS
00702836 Book/CD Pack...............$12.99

18. IRISH SONGS
00703086 Book/Online Audio..........$12.99

19. BLUES STANDARDS
00703087 Book/CD Pack...............$12.99

20. FOLK POP ROCK
00703088 Book/CD Pack...............$12.99

21. HAWAIIAN CLASSICS
00703097 Book/CD Pack...............$12.99

22. ISLAND SONGS
00703098 Book/CD Pack...............$12.99

23. TAYLOR SWIFT – 2ND EDITION
00221966 Book/Online Audio..........$16.99

24. WINTER WONDERLAND
00101871 Book/CD Pack...............$12.99

25. GREEN DAY
00110398 Book/CD Pack...............$14.99

26. BOB MARLEY
00110399 Book/Online Audio..........$14.99

27. TIN PAN ALLEY
00116358 Book/CD Pack...............$12.99

28. STEVIE WONDER
00116736 Book/CD Pack...............$14.99

29. OVER THE RAINBOW & OTHER FAVORITES
00117076 Book/Online Audio..........$14.99

30. ACOUSTIC SONGS
00122336 Book/CD Pack...............$14.99

31. JASON MRAZ
00124166 Book/CD Pack...............$14.99

32. TOP DOWNLOADS
00127507 Book/CD Pack...............$14.99

33. CLASSICAL THEMES
00127892 Book/Online Audio..........$14.99

34. CHRISTMAS HITS
00128602 Book/CD Pack...............$14.99

35. SONGS FOR BEGINNERS
00129009 Book/Online Audio..........$14.99

36. ELVIS PRESLEY HAWAII
00138199 Book/Online Audio..........$14.99

37. LATIN
00141191 Book/Online Audio..........$14.99

38. JAZZ
00141192 Book/Online Audio..........$14.99

39. GYPSY JAZZ
00146559 Book/Online Audio..........$14.99

40. TODAY'S HITS
00160845 Book/Online Audio..........$14.99

HAL•LEONARD®

www.halleonard.com